The NCTE High School Literature Series

■ ■

The NCTE High School Literature Series offers classroom teachers in-depth studies of individual writers. Grounded in theory, each volume focuses on a single author or work and features excerpts from the writer's works, biographical information, and samples of professional literary criticism. Rich in opportunities for classroom discussion and writing assignments that teachers can adapt to their own literature curriculum, each book also offers many examples of student writing.

Volumes in the Series

Tim O'Brien in the Classroom: "This too is true: Stories can save us" (2007), Barry Gilmore and Alexander Kaplan

The Great Gatsby in the Classroom: Searching for the American Dream (2006), David Dowling

Judith Ortiz Cofer in the Classroom: A Woman in Front of the Sun (2006), Carol Jago

Langston Hughes in the Classroom: "Do Nothin' till You Hear from Me" (2006), Carmaletta M. Williams

Amy Tan in the Classroom: "The art of invisible strength" (2005), Renée H. Shea and Deborah L. Wilchek

Raymond Carver in the Classroom: "A Small, Good Thing" (2005), Susanne Rubenstein

Sandra Cisneros in the Classroom: "Do not forget to reach" (2002), Carol Jago

Alice Walker in the Classroom: "Living by the Word" (2000), Carol Jago

Nikki Giovanni in the Classroom: "The same ol danger but a brand new pleasure" (1999), Carol Jago

Staff Editor: Bonny Graham
Interior Design: Jenny Jensen Greenleaf
Cover Design: Jenny Jensen Greenleaf and Tom Jaczak
Cover Photo: Rob Casey

NCTE Stock Number: 44572
ISSN 1525-5786

It is the policy of NCTE in its journals and other publications to provide a forum for the open discussion of ideas concerning the content and the teaching of English and the language arts. Publicity accorded to any particular point of view does not imply endorsement by the Executive Committee, the Board of Directors, or the membership at large, except in announcements of policy, where such endorsement is clearly specified.

Every effort has been made to provide current URLs and email addresses, but because of the rapidly changing nature of the Web, some sites and addresses may no longer be accessible.

Library of Congress Cataloging-in-Publication Data

Bruce, Heather E., 1953–
    Sherman Alexie in the classroom : "This is not a silent movie. Our voices will save our lives" / Heather E. Bruce, Anna E. Baldwin, Christabel Umphrey.
        p. cm. — (The NCTE high school literature series, ISSN 1525-5786)
    Includes bibliographical references.
    ISBN 978-0-8141-4457-2 (pbk.)
    1. Alexie, Sherman, 1966—Study and teaching (Secondary) 2. Indians in literature—Study and teaching (Secondary) 3. Indian authors—United States—Study and teaching (Secondary) 4. American literature—Indian authors—Study and teaching (Secondary) I. Baldwin, Anna E., 1972– II. Umphrey, Christabel, 1976– III. Title.
    PS3551.L35774Z65 2008
    818'.5409—dc22
                                                                          2008016012

Sherman Alexie in the Classr

■ ■

"This is not a silent movie. Our voices will
our lives."

The NCTE High School Literature S

Heather E. Bruce

The University of Montana

Anna E. Baldwin

Arlee High School, Arlee, Montana

Christabel Umphrey

Montana Writing Project

NATIONAL COUNCIL OF TEACHERS OF ENGLISH
1111 W. KENYON ROAD, URBANA, ILLINOIS 61801-1096

Contents

Permission Acknowledgments

■ ■

Excerpts from "Futures" and "13/16," *The Business of Fancydancing* (1992); "On the Amtrak from Boston to New York City" and excerpt from "The Native American Broadcasting System," *The First Indian on the Moon* (1993); excerpts from "Inside Dachau," *The Summer of Black Widows* (1996); all © by Sherman Alexie, reprinted by permission of Hanging Loose Press.

Gustavus Sohon's watercolor of the Battle of Colonel Steptoe, May 17, 1858. From the collection of the Library of Congress.

"Powwow Polaroid" by Sherman Alexie, *Old Shirts and New Skins*, American Indian Studies Center, University of California, Los Angeles. Copyright © 1993 by Sherman Alexie. All rights reserved.

Excerpt from "Sherman Alexie: Irony, Intimacy, and Agency" by David L. Moore. *Cambridge Companion to Native American Literature*, ed. Joy Porter and Kenneth M. Roemer. © 2005 Cambridge University Press. Reprinted with the permission of Cambridge University Press.

Excerpt from "Who Gets to Tell the Stories?" by Elizabeth Cook-Lynn, *Wicazo Sa Review* 9.1 (Spring 1993), pp. 60–64. Reprinted with permission.

"In Response to Elizabeth Cook-Lynn's Pronouncement That I One of the New, Angry (Warriors) Kind of Like Norman Schwarzkopf and Rush Limbaugh" by Sherman Alexie, *Wicazo Sa Review* 9.2 (Autumn 1993). Copyright © 1993. All rights reserved.

Excerpt from "The Exaggeration of Despair in Sherman Alexie's *Reservation Blues*," by Gloria Bird, *Wicazo Sa Review* 11.2 (Fall 1995), pp. 47-52. Reprinted with permission.

Acknowledgments

■ ■

When we began this project, we had no idea how daunting a task we faced. Keeping up with reading the works of Sherman Alexie, much less thinking about how to teach them to our high school and college students, has been a full-time job replete with anxiety, intrigue, awe, respect, laughter, wonder, exhaustion. . . . We first would like to thank Sherman Alexie for all of it. Heather also thanks Rina Moog—although she is no longer with us—for sneaking her in to an NCTE luncheon in Nashville at which Alexie was the sold-out featured speaker and for insisting that she wait as the crowd thinned after his talk to speak with him directly. (Wow!)

Montana is "Big Sky" country for a reason. It takes more than twelve hours to drive across our state and eight hours to drive from the Canadian border into Idaho or Wyoming, our southern neighbors. Fewer than one million people inhabit this expanse. We are far more likely when traveling to encounter gophers, moose, deer, elk, grizzlies, coyotes, wolves, or eagles than people. Human exchange with other teachers is both cherished and difficult across the geographic distances and divides. Although the three of us have never gathered face-to-face, we have managed a rich, lively, committed collaboration, and we thank one another for our hard work and dedication to the project.

We would not have been able to complete this project without the help and support of numerous others. We want to thank our many willing students who provided multiple reality checks, insights, interesting conversations, and honest feedback as they tried out some of the approaches in this text. For their wisdom, insight, literary expertise, and incredible generosity, we thank colleagues at the University of Montana: Casey Charles (English), Debra Magpie Earling (English/Native American Studies), Lynn Itagaki (English), Katie Kane (English), Angelica Lawson (Native American Studies), David L. Moore (English), and Kathryn Shanley (Native American Studies). Anna particularly thanks the administrators of the two districts in which she has taught for allowing her the latitude to teach and try new things, and Tammy Elser, who continually helps her believe in herself. Christa thanks Shirley Goss for taking the time to share what she has been doing with the works of Alexie in her classroom.

Heather additionally thanks the University of Montana for granting a sabbatical leave in part to work on this project; the National Writing Project for granting the opportunity to participate in a professional writing retreat that provided time, editorial support, and Santa Fe inspiration for the work; and especially Tom Fox of the National Writing Project, who is always an enthusiastic mentor/colleague/friend.

We thank Kurt Austin and Bonny Graham at NCTE for their encouragement and support of the project, as well as two anonymous reviewers who gave thoughtful and careful feedback that helped to improve the work. We also thank Bob Hershon at Hanging Loose Press for the panache he exhibited in negotiating permission for us to reprint some of Alexie's poems.

We must also thank those closest to us: Valerie Umphrey, a dedicated professional, great literary resource, and supportive mother and grandmother. It's only because Valerie is a teacher all the hours of her life, in all these areas of her life, that completing projects like this is possible for Christa. Heather also thanks Bruce Adams for unfailing support and for picking up the slack along the way; Dylan and Justin Brunjes for being the best sons in the world; Antoinette Russi-Brunjes, a beloved daughter-in-law; and Mark Medvetz, a generous friend to the end. Anna thanks her mother, Ellie, who has always been utterly supportive of her ideas and endeavors.

Introduction

■ ■

"This is not a silent movie. Our voices will save our lives."

Sherman Alexie is one of the most accomplished and provocative writers to emerge on the American literary scene in the late twentieth century. Incredibly prolific and versatile, Alexie—a Spokane/Coeur d'Alene Indian—is perhaps the best-known Native American writer writing today.[1] Alexie is a fellowship-winning poet, bestselling novelist, award-winning filmmaker, four-time spoken word poetry world champion, stand-up comedian, songwriter, prize-winning short story writer, and 2007 National Book Award winner for Young People's Literature. He published his first book, the book of poems *The Business of Fancydancing*, in 1992 at the age of twenty-six. As of 2008, Alexie has published twenty books of poetry and fiction; written, produced, and directed two feature-length films, *Smoke Signals* and *The Business of Fancydancing*; and published scores of essays and journalistic pieces. His work primarily addresses contemporary issues facing Native Americans. His first young adult novel, *The Absolutely True Diary of a Part-Time Indian*, the National Book Award winner, is a semiautobiographical account about growing up on the Spokane Indian reservation with a variety of medical problems as a "weird," "picked-on," bookish "nerd."

Alexie considers himself first and foremost a poet. His poems have a strong narrative drive and many are prosaic in form. Alexie has been praised as a major lyric voice of our time (Kincaid). He demonstrates considerable knowledge of form and craft through, for example, artfully composed sestinas, sonnets, and the challenging villanelle. He has a poet's obsession with the lyrical, with an ear finely tuned to music and a clear eye for imagery, although he admits in one interview that saying someone "has jeans on" is "big description" for him (qtd. in Bellante and Bellante). He believes that poetry is not a luxury for Indian people; it is key to survival in a world that generally sees Indians as the "noble savage" of the past or irrelevant and invisible in present-day America. As Alexie explains, "I want my literature to concern the daily lives of Indians" (qtd. in Fraser par. 53).

Alexie typically focuses on such topics as broken treaties and manifest destiny, basketball and car wrecks, commodity food and Housing and Urban Development (HUD) houses, smallpox blankets and genocide, violence and alcohol. His work arcs the fullness of Indian humanity—past and present, pain and humor, hunger and survival, love and anger, families and relationships, promises and dreams—broken and fulfilled (Brill; Goebel). His poetry and fiction depict an "uneasy cross-cultural mix, or confusion," as critic Ron McFarland says, commenting on Alexie's emblematic usage of simple syntax and understated, colloquial diction represented in the opening stanza of Alexie's poem "Futures" from *The Business of Fancy-dancing*:

> We lived in the HUD house
> for fifty bucks a month.
> Those were the good times.
> ANNIE GREEN SPRINGS WINE
> was a dollar a bottle.
> My uncles always came over
> to eat stew and fry bread
> to get drunk in the sweatlodge
> to spit and piss in the fire.

"The HUD house and the sweat lodge, cheap wine and fry bread, drunkenness and sacred, purifying ritual" demonstrate many of Alexie's recurrent themes (McFarland, *Dictionary* 5). His writing gives voice to contemporary Indian life in America and forges hope for Indian recognition and survival: "This is not a silent movie. Our voices will save our lives" ("Reservation Drive-In," *First Indian on the Moon* 17).

Although Alexie imagines his ideal audience as "reservation kids"—whom he believes to be influenced mainly by white-dominated popular culture—he is acutely aware that his primary audience is non-Indian. Many of Alexie's stories, poems, and films feature young adult Indian characters whom he draws on repeatedly, in addition to characters based in the past and in modern-day culture. He frequently animates his work with references to television, film, historic events, and music to capture Indian youngsters' attention and to speak in their language (Cline; Fraser; Spencer), hoping they might recognize themselves in his work, understand it, and be motivated to revolutionary counteraction; however, he also appeals to a wider readership by doing so. For example, Alexie invigorates incarnations of Christopher Columbus, Crazy Horse, George Armstrong Custer, and Buffalo Bill to interact in mythical ways with icons such as John Wayne, Jimi Hendrix, Arnold Schwarzenegger, Marlon Brando, and the Lone Ranger. This outrageous juxtaposition of personalities creates "a sort of postmodernist fantasy" (McFarland, *Dictionary* 6) that dismantles non-Indians' romanticized nostalgic image of the American Indian so often glorified in the media and imprinted in the American psyche.

Alexie challenges both malevolent and benign stereotypes of Indians and complicates simple perceptions about Native peoples now living in America (Goebel). He is driven to rewrite the prevalent version of American history, "which barely acknowledges the violent colonization and subsequent massacres of Indians by European settlers" (Grassian 11). A member of Generation X, Alexie challenges readers, through an indigenous rhetoric of race, to understand Indians in a predominantly postmodern, televisual world and to reflect on historic and persistent mistreatment of Native peoples.

Alexie is a master satirist who provides poignant and humorous access to his described Indian worlds through rich layers of "parodic antiformalism" (Lincoln, "Futuristic Hip" 267). Most of his work can be read as a product of his anger and wit and is intended to make a vivid social point, which, combined with his desire to correct wrong through ridicule, "marks him as a satirist" (McFarland, *Dictionary* 4). He cleverly exercises irony and satire as comedic counterpoints to smooth the sharp edges of the social and political commentary that punctuate his poems and stories and to disperse the anger that invigorates his tales of Indian life in modern-day America. The ironic non sequitur is one of Alexie's favored vehicles for delivering humorous punch lines (McFarland, *Dictionary* 6).

Most of our students, both Indian and non-Indian, find Sherman Alexie's work intriguing. His popular culture references, which make his work especially accessible to adolescents, help to put readers on common ground. They appreciate his maverick charm and his Comedy Channel–like worlds. As one critic describes Alexie, the "reader enters the land of MTV and renascent AIM: a cartoon Pocahontas meets Beavis and Butt-head at the forest's edge, Sitting Bull takes on Arnold Schwarzenegger at Wounded Knee '73. The Last Real Indian has a few last words" (Lincoln, "Futuristic Hip" 267). Our students go for this rebellious synthesis. Alexie's experiments in genre, form, and irony also appeal to our students' postmodern sensibilities. Because many of our students feel rather hopeless in a world troubled by chaos, violence, corporate and political scandal, environmental devastation, and war, Alexie's blend of anger, humorous disregard, and imaginative creativity gives them reason to hope for survival in a dangerous world, gives them reason to speak up and be counted.

This book is organized to make it as accessible as possible as a guide to teachers who want to learn about Alexie and teach his work. We structured chapters by focusing on significant genres of his work while trying to do justice to his wide-ranging accomplishments and exceptional productivity, knowing we could not address the whole of his oeuvre (and all this from a writer who only recently turned forty).

We imagined as we wrote that readers would read for background introduction Chapter 1, "Where Life and Art Intersect," which includes a biography of Alexie and an overview of themes in his work. A companion website, http://alexie.website.googlepages.com, addresses issues readers frequently encounter while reading Native American literature. Remaining chapters are organized as individual units so they can be used independently of others. Nonetheless, overlapping themes emerge.

Chapter 2, "*Smoke Signals*: Visual Literacy and Multimodal Texts," addresses Alexie's interest in television and film and leads teachers through instructional viewing of Alexie's first feature-length film, *Smoke Signals*, based on the short story "This Is What It Means to Say Phoenix, Arizona" from the collection *The Lone Ranger and Tonto Fistfight in Heaven*.

Chapter 3, "*The Lone Ranger and Tonto Fistfight in Heaven*: Alexie and History," takes teachers through reading, research, and writing activities designed to help students understand Alexie's exercise of humor, historical references, and Native American history.

Chapter 4, "Slam! Writing and Performing Poetry," introduces Alexie's prowess as both a literary and a performance poet while helping teachers develop students' dramatic literacy through writing and performing poetry, with special attention paid to teaching the poetic forms of the sestina and the villanelle.

Chapter 5, "*Reservation* (Sings the) *Blues*," guides teachers in helping students understand the musical underpinnings of Alexie's first novel, *Reservation Blues*. The chapter provides reading guidance to help students navigate the nonlinear organization of time in the work.

Chapter 6, "Taking a Critical Stance," excerpts analyses of Alexie's work from professional literary criticism and guides teachers in helping students write critical reviews. Chapter 6 should enable both teachers' and students' understanding of prominent themes and features of Alexie's writing. For those least familiar with Alexie's work and Native American literature in general, studying Chapter 6 along with Chapter 1 will help build useful interpretive knowledge prior to teaching.

Chapter 7, "*Flight* and *The Absolutely True Diary of a Part-Time Indian*: Post 9/11 Reconciliation," examines Alexie's questions about tribalism following the September 11, 2001, terrorist attacks and provides reading and writing exercises that address the negative aspects of tribalism and the hopefulness of reconciliation.

Note

1. A note about terminology: diverse terminology is currently in use to refer to "Native Americans." We use the terms *Native American, indigenous, American Indian,* and *Indian* interchangeably. The term *American Indian* most accurately refers specifically to the tribal peoples in the United States who hold treaty rights and sovereign status (see Grande 8). Sherman Alexie dismisses the term *Native American* as meaningless, a product of liberal white guilt. "I'm an Indian," he says. "I'll only use Native American in mixed company" (Himmelsbach).

1 Where Life and Art Intersect

■■■■■■■■■■■■■■■■■■■■■■■■■■■■■■■■■■■■■

Sherman J. Alexie Jr., a Spokane-Couer d'Alene Indian whose mother, Lillian Agnes Cox Alexie, is Spokane and father, Sherman Joseph Alexie Sr., was Coeur d'Alene, grew up in eastern Washington on the Spokane Reservation in Wellpinit, a town of about 1,100 people, most of whom are Spokane tribal members. The reservation is about fifty miles northwest of the city of Spokane and is the second largest in the state. Alexie now lives in Seattle, Washington, and is married to Diane Alexie, who is of Hidatsa, Ho-Chunk (Winnebago), and Pottawatomi descent. They have two sons (Hollrah).

Childhood

Born on October 7, 1966, Alexie had hydrocephalus, a life-threatening condition sometimes called "water on the brain." At the age of six months, he underwent risky surgery to correct the malady even though doctors did not expect him to live or, if he did, only with severe mental handicaps. Alexie has never demonstrated any evidence of brain damage; however, throughout his childhood he suffered side effects from the surgery, which included an enlarged skull, severe seizures, and uncontrollable nightly incontinence. Nevertheless, Alexie taught himself to read at a very early age and was devouring novels like John Steinbeck's *The Grapes of Wrath* by age five even though he admits he only understood the last chapter (Cline par. 3). He had read every book in the Wellpinit School library by the time he was twelve (Grassian 2).

As a result of his physical deformities and interest in books, Alexie was frequently taunted, ostracized, and beaten up by other children on the reservation. "You get treated like shit as a people for hundreds of years, and you get good at treating other people like shit. You get taught very well how to oppress," says Alexie now (qtd. in Wilton par. 3). He turned to humor to fend off the harassment of his peers. Alexie explains his defense: "You can't run as fast or throw a punch if you're laughing" (qtd. in Pabst par. 30). Discovering in humor a source of both protection and empowerment, Alexie abundantly exercises his acerbic humor and wit in all his writing.

Alexie says that contrary to how it looks, humor does not come easy. He works hard at the ideas in his humor. "Because I'm funny, people think it's not insightful or not thought out or that I'm being flippant when I'm very serious about being funny. I'm very careful and I know what I'm saying and the effect I want" (qtd. in Torrez par. 16). He constructs humor like "a serious poem" (qtd. in Pabst par. 29).

Adolescence

Alexie attended tribal school in Wellpinit through the eighth grade. After he found his mother's name written in a textbook he was assigned at Wellpinit School, he decided to attend all-white Reardon High School, about an hour's drive from his home. In his largely autobiographical first young adult novel, *The Absolutely True Diary of a Part-Time Indian*, Alexie illuminates:

> [I opened the book and] saw this written on the inside cover: This Book Belongs to Agnes Adams. . . . MY MOTHER! And

Adams is her *maiden* name. . . . [S]he was still an Adams when she wrote her name in that book. And she was thirty when she gave birth to me . . . so that means I was staring at a . . . book that was at least thirty years older than I was. . . . My school and my tribe are so poor and sad that we have to study from the same dang books our parents studied from. That is absolutely the saddest thing in the world. (31)

Alexie believed he would get a better education at Reardon High even though he would be the only Indian there "except for the mascot" (http://www.fallsapart.com/biography.html, par. 3). At Reardon, Alexie excelled academically and became a star player on the basketball team. He reflects on his experiences:

On the rez I was abused. I was picked on and beat up. I was low, low, low, in the structure. But then I left the rez. . . . I still lived on the rez; I just went to another high school. I was just a really weird kid. Different. And I got abused. But it's funny, all of those qualities that made me a geek on the rez—I was academic, talked a lot, I was ambitious—all this kind of stuff that made me odd on the rez made me popular at the white school. It was a school of over-achievers. I was a jock but I was also in drama club. I was also in Future Farmers of America, which is the biggest group of geeks on the planet. So, I sort of fit in a lot of different places. . . . I was captain of the basketball team, I was prom king. (qtd. in Torrez par. 12)

Alexie found an appreciative audience for his humor and eccentricities at Reardon. He was elected class president and was a member of a championship debate team.

After Alexie graduated with honors from Reardon High in 1985, he attended Gonzaga University, a Jesuit college in Spokane, on a scholarship. Alexie was not enamored with the social environment at Gonzaga, where the students were predominantly white and privileged. In his view, the atmosphere at Gonzaga was elitist. His studies deteriorated and he was drinking heavily, so he dropped out of school, moved to Seattle, and worked in a restaurant as a busboy. On his twenty-first birthday, he was robbed at knifepoint, had an epiphany, and decided to change the direction of his life by going back to school, this time to Washington State University in Pullman (Grassian 2–3).

College

Although Alexie originally planned to be a medical doctor when he returned to school, he kept fainting in human anatomy class. Needless to say, recurrent fainting did not bode well for his future in medicine. He dropped anatomy and transferred into a poetry-writing workshop because it was the only other class open during that time block. In the writing workshop, Alexie read for the first time a collection of Native American poetry, *Songs from This Earth on Turtle's Back*, an anthology of contemporary American Indian poetry edited by Joseph Bruchac. Reading Native American poetry was enlightening for Alexie, who recalls, "I opened it up and—oh my gosh—I saw my life in poems and stories for the first time" (qtd. in Highway par. 69). One poem in particular, written by Paiute poet Adrian Louis, was "revolutionary and revelatory" for him. It contained the line "I'm in the reservation of my mind." Alexie recalls,

> For me, that was like, "In the beginning . . ." It was, "Because I could not stop for death, death kindly stopped for me. . . ." It was, " I sing the body electric. . . ." It was all that and more. It was the first line I ever read in any work, any fiction anywhere that ever applied to something I knew. Literally, it was this flash of lightning, roll of thunder, Bert Parks parking, Bob Barker barking, where I understood everything that I ever wanted to

be. At that moment. When I read that line. It was really like that, like a light switch. And at that moment I knew I wanted to be a writer. (qtd. in Ivry par. 2)

He knew he wanted to be a writer and began to write poems (qtd. in Highway par. 72).

Alex Kuo, his poetry instructor, was captivated by Alexie's work and encouraged him to pursue a career in writing (Grassian 3). Only three credits shy of a bachelor's degree, Alexie left Washington State to write full time, but the university awarded him a degree in American studies in 1995 after he had published several books and received relative renown (Brill). Shortly after leaving the university, Alexie received the Washington State Arts Commission Poetry Fellowship and the National Endowment for the Arts Poetry Fellowship. During this time, he worked at a high school in Spokane as an administrator, continuing to write and publish poetry. On the day of publication of *The Business of Fancydancing*, Alexie gave up drinking alcohol and has been sober ever since (*Nativelandz* par. 5).

Turning Life into Art

Much of Alexie's poetry and fiction takes place on the Spokane Indian Reservation where he grew up. He draws frequently from his own life experiences to create his characters. Plot events habitually mirror those that have occurred in Alexie's life and in those that are commonly contextualized in Native American history.

Life on an Indian reservation can be pretty bleak. Alexie explains that until bingo halls and casinos opened on his reservation, 90 percent of the people were unemployed (Highway). Estimates suggest that alcohol and drugs are responsible for more than half of the deaths on reservations. Indian scholar Jace Weaver explains:

> The average yearly income is half the poverty level, and over half of all Natives are unemployed. On some reservations, unemployment runs as high as 85–90 percent. Health statistics chronically rank Natives at or near the bottom. Male life expectancy is forty-four years, and female is forty-seven. . . . Substance abuse, suicide, crime, and violence are major problems among both urban and reservation populations. (11)

Not surprisingly, readers will encounter in Sherman Alexie's work a good deal of poverty, profanity, risky sex, alcohol and drug abuse, violence, and death, which may cause problems for some readers.

Alexie is unwavering in his desire to help his audience think about the issues he writes about, even if his positions on these issues are radical, disturbing, and confrontational (Grassian 14). He urges us to understand that the at-risk conditions common to peoples living under siege conditions persist not because children and families have problems, but rather because their problems have been consciously and historically produced by and through systems of colonization: "a multidimensional force underwritten by Western Christianity, defined by white supremacy, and fueled by global capitalism" (Grande 19). Alexie doesn't want to write books that entertain or offer a form of escape: "I don't want to write books that provide people with that. I want books that challenge, anger, and possibly offend" (qtd. in Cline par. 2).

Poetry = Survival

"Poetry = Anger × Imagination"
—"Indian Education," *Old Shirts and New Skins*

"Survival = Anger × Imagination"
—"Imagining the Reservation," *The Lone Ranger and Tonto Fistfight in Heaven*

Anger and humor are in constant tension in Sherman Alexie's work. Alexie equates writing poetry with survival, both the product of "Anger × Imagination." "Imagination is the only weapon on the reservation," he asserts ("Imagining the Reservation," *The Lone Ranger and Tonto Fistfight in Heaven* [*LRTFIN*] 150). He suggests that art is a synthesis of imagination coupled with anger and that such art intervenes in violence and generates survival. Mere imagination or creativity is not enough; it must be multiplied by outrage, which for Alexie is the result of the historical mistreatment and current marginalization of American Indians by mainstream, predominantly white Americans. Alexie thinks that imagination fueled by anger can counteract the effects of outrage by offering hope and aggressively challenging the status quo. To challenge mainstream culture, Alexie realizes, one needs to be passionately, even furiously inspired. There is no way to empowerment except through rage transformed constructively via art. Poetry is the imaginative vehicle by which anger can be transformed into something productive—survival (Grassian 30).

Alexie writes about the ongoing genocide and oppression of Native American peoples using a sharp "comedic style and ironic attitude," which allow him both to educate his audience and to critique U.S. policies that perpetuate the contemporary plight of American Indians in ways more palatable to his varied audiences (D. Moore 297). There is anger tempered by pride, as well as desperation tempered by humor and affection. Humor ameliorates devastating situations and makes poverty and despondency bearable (Grassian 77). Alexie says about his exercise of humor,

> I've learned that humor can be very serious. If you have people laughing, you can talk about very difficult subjects. I use it as an aesthetic—I suppose I should say anesthetic—and also to be profane and blasphemous. There's nothing I like more than laughing at other people's idea of the sacred. (Wyrick par. 10)

Alexie portrays American Indians as battered but resilient survivors of an unacknowledged American genocide who continually struggle against the culture that stripped them of property, pride, and their indigenous culture. It is tough to make jokes about genocide, alcoholism, and poverty, yet, as Kenneth Lincoln proclaims in "Futuristic Hip Indian," Alexie uses "poetic anger, ribald love, and whipsaw humor" and succeeds (268).

Alexie's fierce pride and brilliant anger erupt in poems like "13/16," which refers to the blood quantum Indians require for tribal enrollment: "I cut myself into sixteen equal pieces / keep thirteen and feed the other three / to the dogs, who have also grown / tired of U.S. Commodities, white cans / black letters translated into Spanish. / Does this mean I have to learn / the language to eat? / Lester FallsApart asks . . ." (*The Business of Fancydancing* 16). His writing blends into something that both terrifies and comforts.

Alexie's work is "a rich mix of seeming opposites: spiritual and prosaic, mythic and contemporary, hilarious and sorrowful. A deep vein of sadness is often apparent under his characters' constant stream of witticisms[,] . . . a combination of lively black humor and great seriousness" (Wilton par. 6). Although tragic anger punctuates much of Alexie's work, humor is its central mechanism of delivery. As he puts it in "The Approximate Size of My Favorite Tumor," "laughter saves [us] from pain. . . . [H]umor [is] an antiseptic that clean[s] the deepest of personal wounds" (*LRTFIH* 164).

Alexie explores what seems to be his love/hate relationship with the reservation. It is not his intent to portray reservation Indians as helpless, poverty-stricken alcoholics, although many of his characters possess those features, and a number of other Native American writers, as well as some Spokane people, have chided him for focusing on the negative, for "airing dirty laundry" (see Bird and Cook-Lynn in Chapter 6). Alexie's work portrays love for the strength of its residents, who struggle to survive amidst abysmal, nearly "Third World" conditions, while he condemns the conditions themselves and how those conditions often poison and demolish Indian people's pride and dignity. Alexie details the desperation of reservation life, noting how impoverished conditions help forge a strong community—held together by what destroys it, alcohol and poverty, and by what helps it survive, humor and television (Grassian 20–21). Alexie's work reflects the ambiguities inherent in survival against enormous odds (16).

Alexie frequently uses peripatetic Spokane Indian characters who walk symbolically through his poems and stories, morphing to fit varying plots. These include the outcast storyteller Thomas Builds-the-Fire; the homeless alcoholic Vietnam veteran Lester FallsApart; the angry and violent alcoholic Victor Joseph; and the easygoing but unfortunate Junior Polatkin. In both his poetry and fiction, Alexie weaves in historical fact that depends on irony for critical effect. These facts often appear in the guise of archetypal historic characters such as the antitheticals Buffalo Bill and Crazy Horse, George Armstrong Custer and Columbus, and popular culture characters such as the Lone Ranger, Tonto, Jimi Hendrix, Fred Astaire, and John Wayne. Alexie places these historical and media figures in contemporary contexts for transformative purposes (Grassian 26). For readers to comprehend the irony that motivates Alexie's characterizations and plot turns, an understanding of these historic events and characters is necessary; otherwise much of his humor comes across as sadistic. Our students generally need to build background knowledge in order to see that Alexie is using humor, particularly irony, and imagination to dispel anger and to survive, not just telling "sad stories of Indian failure," as several of our students have complained.

Memory and Place: Making Connections

In preparation for some of the difficult work Alexie asks his readers to do, we have used a visualization, mapping, and writing activity that helps our students begin to think about the importance of place and memory in Alexie's work. We pass out drawing paper and an array of colored pencils, markers, chalk, and crayons. We first ask students to think about a place that in younger years was special to them and why it was important: "Where was this place? How large or small? What was the geography of the place? What objects do you recall? What colors, light, temperature can you remember? What did you like to do there? Who was with you? What were the smells, sights, sounds, flavors?" After giving students several minutes to think about and visualize a place, we ask them to draw a map that illustrates the place as they recall it. We encourage as much detail as possible and ask them to label the items they draw (e.g., "tall Ponderosa pine tree at the northwest corner of the playground) and code them for personal meaning (e.g., "At recess it becomes Fort Pine Ridge where fourth- and fifth-grade boys came to do battle—as cowboys vs. Indians"). We might play soothing music or nature/environment sound tracks or gritty hip-hop or urban cityscape-style music to backdrop the activity and to emphasize tone and mood created by place. In a block session of ninety minutes, we like to give students about half the time to draw, label, and code so they don't feel rushed (with forty-five-minute periods, this activity can be easily divided into two classes). When it seems as though a good number in the class have finished their maps, we ask them to look at the map as a prewriting experience and then "to set a scene" and write about a specific experience they recall that occurred in that place. We give students the starting prompt, "One day at [Ft. Pine Ridge], I . . ."

Students generally become very involved in the drawing and writing, and often keep working after we have called "Time." Following the activity, we ask writers to hold up the map for everyone to see and to tell the story of their map. Some will read what they have written out loud; others hold the map up for view and provide an oral retelling of the story(-ies) behind the map. We listen intently and give feedback to the writer about a particularly strong aspect of the storytelling. This, too, is an important element of the activity because the sharing of place and memory helps to build classroom community and camaraderie.[1]

This activity also helps students begin to make connections between place and memory, a connection so vivid in Alexie's work. It becomes a touchstone experience that readers can draw on continually. Occasionally we draw maps of Alexie's poems and stories to connect his sense of place with our own. Because many of our students have grown up in small towns in rural areas, it is not unusual for two or more students to create a map of the same place but with two entirely different stories. This creates a useful connection to Alexie. When this happens, we find Alexie's frequently anthologized poem, "On the Amtrak from Boston to New York City" (*The First Indian on the Moon*), a good one to examine for the ways in which multiple competing stories might be told about a place. We read the poem and discuss the anger and pain that arise in trying to sort through discrepancies. Our own mapping activity gives students the background knowledge to understand Alexie's point and helps them delve into the complexities.

On the Amtrak from Boston to New York City

The white woman across the aisle from me says, "Look,
look at all the history, that house
on the hill there is over two hundred years old,"
as she points out the window past me

into what she has been taught. I have learned
little more about American history during my few days
back East than what I expected and far less
of what we should all know of the tribal stories

whose architecture is 15,000 years older
than the corners of the house that sits
museumed on the hill. "Walden Pond,"
the woman on the train asks, "Did you see Walden Pond?"

and I don't have a cruel enough heart to break
her own by telling her there are five Walden Ponds
on my little reservation out West
and at least a hundred more surrounding Spokane,

the city I pretend to call my home. "Listen,"
I could have told her. "I don't give a shit
about Walden. I know the Indians were living stories
around that pond before Walden's grandparents were born

and before his grandparents' grandparents were born.
I'm tired of hearing about Don-fucking-Henley saving it, too,
because that's redundant. If Don Henley's brothers and sisters
and mothers and fathers hadn't come here in the first place

then nothing would need to be saved."
But I didn't say a word to the woman about Walden
Pond because she smiled so much and seemed delighted
that I thought to bring her an orange juice
back from the food car. I respect elders
of every color. All I really did was eat
my tasteless sandwich, drink my Diet Pepsi
and nod my head whenever the woman pointed out

another little piece of her country's history
while I, as all Indians have done
since this war began, made plans
for what I would do and say the next time
somebody from the enemy thought I was one of their own.

Many of our students find this, and much of Alexie's work, difficult because of the inherent accusations Alexie is making about
Euro-American colonization and occupation of Indian lands and
the resulting genocide of America's indigenous peoples. However,
we, like Alexie, think the ongoing oppression of America's first
peoples has continued long enough. Our only hope for social
and political change lies in educating ourselves and our students
and in dealing with the complexity of such issues. Alexie gives us
food for thought and means for discussing these concerns with
students, who might in turn be motivated to use their energies to
take up different approaches toward Indian matters and toward
ongoing conquest, war, and colonization undertakings in the future. We talk with our students about "white guilt,"[2] a problem
with which many of our students struggle while reading Alexie.
His humor gives them ways to contemplate the difficulties and to
find some strategic resolutions to these problems.

Other Activities

We have also used ideas developed by Linda Christensen in her marvelous resource *Reading, Writing, and Rising Up: Teaching about Social Justice and the Power of the Written Word.* We have discovered that our students' understanding of the issues raised by Alexie are greatly illuminated when we adapt Christensen's classroom-tested suggestions. In particular, we have used her ideas for prompting students to write the story of their names (1–13) and her ideas for prompting students to write "I Am From" bio-poems modeled after the poem by George Ella Lyon (18–22). Alexie has written an "I am" poem himself, which provides students with a model:

> [Excerpt from "The Native American Broadcasting System," *First Indian on the Moon* 9.]

> I am the essence of powwow, I am
> toilets without paper, I am fry bread
> in sawdust, I am bull dung
> on rodeo grounds at the All-Indian
> Rodeo and Horse Show, I am

> the essence of powwow, I am
> video games with braids, I am spit
> from toothless mouths, I am turquoise
> and bootleg whiskey, both selling
> for twenty bucks a swallow, I am

> the essence of powwow, I am
> fancydancers in flannel, I am host drum
> amplified, I am *Fuck you*
> *don't come back* and *Leave me*

> *the last hard drink.* I am
> the essence of powwow, I am the dream

you lace your shoes with, I am
the lust between your toes, I am
the memory you feel across the bottom
of your feet whenever you walk too close.

Notes

1. We wish to thank Judy Blunt for introducing us to this activity.

2. There are numerous resources for helping white teachers and students work through "white guilt" and develop antiracist perspectives. Good starting resources include:

Derman-Sparks, Louise, and Carol Brunson Phillips. *Teaching/Learning Anti-Racism: A Developmental Approach.* New York: Teachers College P, 1997.

Howard, Gary R. *We Can't Teach What We Don't Know: White Teachers, Multiracial Schools.* New York: Teachers College P, 1999.

Kivel, Paul. *Uprooting Racism: How White People Can Work for Racial Justice.* Gabriola Island, BC: New Society, 1996.

2 *Smoke Signals*: Visual Literacy and Multimodal Texts

■ ■

Sherman Alexie admits he has always loved movies. When he was ten years old, his family spent $1,000 on a VCR, significantly more than their monthly income. Alexie explains, "I love movies more than I love books, and believe me I love books more than I love every human being, except the dozen or so people in my life who love movies and books as much as I do" (*Smoke Signals: A Screenplay* vii). His passion is evident in his numerous stories and poems filled with references to TV and film. He knows what a powerful influence they have; what he has seen has shaped how he views the world. As a result, it is unsurprising that Alexie works in the medium himself. His first feature film, *Smoke Signals*, is based on his story "This Is What It Means to Say Phoenix, Arizona" from *The Lone Ranger and Tonto Fistfight in Heaven*.

Smoke Signals is the result of a collaborative effort between Alexie and Chris Eyre, a Cheyenne and Arapaho, who directed the film. The film Eyre and Alexie created, like all of Alexie's poetry and stories, expands our ideas of what Indians look like and reminds us that Indians are not a people that existed only in some distant Wild West version of the past. All the major elements of the film make it a strong piece to use to introduce students to postcolonial issues. In numerous interviews and essays, Alexie has made it clear that he is interested in truthfully portraying the community and lifestyle (and all its social, political, economic, and cultural aspects) that he was familiar with growing up on the Spokane Reservation. Much of this way of life was in response and resistance to the lingering colonial influence on Indian people.

Alexie thinks that many Americans have gained most of their understanding of Native Americans from what they have seen in the movies. Too often American film has dished out "endless looping reels of Anglo cowboys defeating Indian villains replayed at drive-ins and on TV" (Gillan 99). The result is that "[a]s these heroes subdue dark Indians hour after hour, they convey the message of Indian inferiority, which gains strength and legitimacy with time, repetition, and syndication" (99). Alexie knows American cinema has work to do when it comes to producing films that more accurately portray American Indians, which is one of his motivations for writing screenplays. For example, Alexie admits that he loved John Ford's *The Searchers*:

> I rooted for John Wayne . . . even though I knew he was going to kill his niece because she had been "soiled" by the Indians. Hell, I rooted for John Wayne because I understood why he wanted to kill his niece. I hated those Indians just as much as John Wayne did. I mean, jeez, they had kidnapped Natalie Wood . . . who certainly didn't deserve to be nuzzled, nibbled, or nipped by some Indian warrior, especially an Indian warrior who only spoke in monosyllables and whose every movement was accompanied by ominous music. ("I Hated Tonto" par. 11–13).

Alexie rooted for Wayne because he did not recognize those Indians. "I wasn't those Indians; I wasn't running around in a loincloth. I wasn't vicious. I wasn't some sociopath with war paint" (qtd. in Mabrey par. 15). Unfortunately, much of the rest of

America does recognize these film portrayals, and others like them, as "real" Indians.

Film is a powerful medium with intense and long-lasting influence. Rennard Strickland recounts a story about the set of another of John Ford's Westerns: "The cameras stop. The Navajo actors dismount and take off their Sioux war bonnets. One of the film crew says to the Indians, 'That was wonderful, you did it just right.' An Indian actor replies, 'Yeah, we did it just like we saw it in the movies'" (par. 1). We need new stories when even Indians are learning how to be Indian by watching movies. We agree with filmmaker Oliver Stone, who says "the stories we like to believe or know about ourselves, are part of the ammunition we take with us into the everyday battles of how we define ourselves and how we act toward other people" (qtd. in Carnes 306). It is increasingly important to think critically about the kind of stories we view on film. *Smoke Signals*, the first movie written, directed, and even nearly entirely acted by Native Americans, provides important (re)vision in reversing this trend by including a diversity of Indian personalities (Mabrey). *Smoke Signals* is full of culturally specific details and there are no non-Native characters central to the story. Watching the film and discussing what they see happening on screen gives students an opportunity to increase their familiarity with American Indian issues.

Although *Smoke Signals* is worth viewing just for the storytelling and film production, we want students to view the film critically as well. We spend a few days building a critical framework that students can work from before we actually watch the film. Gore Vidal writes, "In the end, he who screens the history makes the history" (81). Because we want students to think about the validity of this statement, we move quickly from reader-response work (which provides important opportunities for students to examine their personal knowledge and experience base) to working with a postcolonial lens so they can investigate how an individual or group's daily life and ideology are shaped by what they see and hear from those in positions of power. More specifically, this approach helps guide students to examine how colonization has affected Indian identity (both within Indian communities and outside them) by thinking about the lasting consequences of outsiders with significant ability to influence everything from a community's economics to the stories the people grow up hearing about themselves.

Previewing

Because Alexie has talked and written at length about wanting his work to move audiences away from narrow and stereotypical views of Native people, a view that Native people had very little influence in shaping, one way to frame the film so students think about these issues as they view it is to read Alexie's poem "My Heroes Have Never Been Cowboys" from *First Indian on the Moon* and discuss Indian stereotypes by looking at some of the ways Indians are portrayed in society.

Before we read the poem, we want students to begin thinking about the ideas and history that Alexie references. We take a word or phrase from each stanza of the poem to use as a writing prompt, read the stanza number and phrase, and ask students to write the corresponding number on their paper and two or three sentences that come to mind when they hear each word or phrase. These are the prompt words we have used for each stanza in this exercise:

1. Columbus
2. cowboys and Indians
3. "how the West was won"
4. cowboy shows
5. heroes
6. "Win their hearts and minds and you win the war."
7. old westerns

8. translated from the American
9. American dream
10. God
11. John Wayne
12. home movies
13. life change
14. "We're all extras"

This is an informal exercise meant to be completed quickly. Its purpose is to gather initial ideas, experiences, and impressions. What personal connections do students have to these ideas? What do they know about the history that is connected to the words and phrases? After time to reflect and write, each student reads aloud some of what he or she has written, moving through the whole list at once (so two students might read from number one, followed by two from number two, and so on) until everyone in the class has shared something and we have covered all the stanzas. Then we read Alexie's poem "My Heroes Have Never Been Cowboys" and look for differences and similarities in the connotations of the words between those of the class and Alexie's. Sometimes, rather than taking on the poem as a whole, we read the poem stanza by stanza, sharing our associations, then reading Alexie's corresponding stanza and discussing similarities and differences in each section.

Many students will miss important references. Among others, they'll run into Randolph Scott, the 1940s film cowboy-hero; Tom Mix, whose over 300 films were nearly all silent but did much to define the Western genre; "These Boots Are Made for Walking," a song students might recognize but will likely associate with Jewel or Jessica Simpson rather than Nancy Sinatra; the term *manifest destiny* and the idea that it was God's will that the United States should stretch from sea to sea; and John Wayne, possibly the most well-known onscreen, Indian-fighting cowboy. So be prepared to offer a few sentences about these references or give students the job of looking into the topics beforehand so they are poised to read with the necessary background information.

Once we work our way through the poem comparing our own historical connections with Alexie's associations, we then read it once aloud in its entirety while students underline parts that connect in some way to things they have written about. Next, we listen to Willie Nelson's song "My Heroes Have Always Been Cowboys." As students listen to the song, we ask them to think about ways in which Willie Nelson's impression of cowboys and life and culture in the West differ from Alexie's. We challenge students to write reflectively about where their own ideas fit:

> What do Alexie and Nelson indicate about their experiences and the stories they heard about the West as children? Did you see any similarities? differences? Which version is more familiar to you? Why do you think this is? Did you ever watch shows about cowboys and Indians when you were younger? Was it a game you played? Were you "Pursuin' the life of my high-ridin' heroes," like Nelson, or did Alexie's line "all us little Skins fought on the same side against the cowboys in our minds" resonate more with you?

Even though the cowboy and Indian films of the era Alexie and Nelson write about are significantly before the time of today's students, many are still familiar with the genre and grew up surrounded by the same imagery.

Both versions resonate with our students, many of whom live on an Indian reservation in Montana. Austin remembered "playing cowboys and Indians" and said, "I was always an Indian, I think . . . because I am an Indian. As I got older, I got confused. . . . I didn't know you could be both cowboy and Indian." In Montana some of the best cowboys are Indians, which shows there can be overlap in the two dramatically different ideologies. For Danna, Alexie's words made sense because she was from the reservation and was familiar with the ideology his poem expressed, but Nelson's song seemed familiar too because she grew up on horses, living a lifestyle that resembled the one he wrote about. She knew she had played cowboys and Indians when she was younger but confessed, "I don't remember who won." For many of our students, neither Nelson nor Alexie seem to get it just right. Or they both do. Helping students examine the contrasting viewpoints complicates their understanding of American history. After the class has had time to write and has discussed the stories about American history they heard when they were younger, we push them to think about ways colonialism has influenced Alexie's ideas and their own: Were there any moments when Alexie's poem made you rethink what you'd learned about the history of the West? In what specific ways does the poem resist the accepted story of "how the West was won"? Were there any topics raised in Alexie's poem that you didn't know much about? How is Alexie's discussion about America different from what you've heard in movies or read in books? Who has influenced what you know about this country and its history? What stake do they have in what version of the story you know? Why does your understanding of the past matter?

Once they begin looking critically at various interpretations of history, some students are quick to find inconsistencies. For

Danna, Alexie's version is "the way it is. Indians had their territory, identity, dreams ripped away from them," but then at the same time, "Cowboys never seemed to be in the wrong." Raising students' awareness of the many competing narratives as well as having them think about who is telling the stories and how that influences the telling help prepare them to understand what Alexie and Eyre were working against as they created *Smoke Signals*. Many students have the background to understand this, though they may not be aware of it without prompting.

After reading both Alexie's antiheroic and Nelson's heroic visions of cowboys, Melinda shared one of her experiences:

> When I was little I remember watching some old westerns with my family. They would laugh at times in the movie that weren't really supposed to be funny. I would laugh with them even though I didn't understand why they were laughing. I came to realize sometime later why they were laughing. The Indians weren't really Indians and the cowboys didn't have to reload their guns or even have to aim to bring down three Indians at a time.

Since images like the ones Melinda writes about are still the most familiar portrayals of Indians much of society has to draw on, *Smoke Signals* is a valuable resource for expanding students' ideas about Native Americans.

After we look at the poem and song lyrics, a second brief previewing activity we do is to help students think through stereotypes about Indians that exist in American cultural lore. We tell students before this activity to bring in a picture or image of an Indian. We want them to spend some time paying attention to where images of Indians appear and how they are portrayed. Students may gather images from books, magazines, online, advertisements, video and audio clips, products they buy or clothing they own, or whatever else they wish. Students who live in an Indian community may bring in actual photographs of friends or family members, though we do not suggest this at first. If you work with American Indian students and no one chooses this option on their own, why no one does so sparks interesting discussion. Images of "real" Indians provide remarkable contrast with the Indian art prints, American Spirit cigarette or Red Man chew ads, or Atlanta Braves baseball hats students otherwise collect.[1]

When students bring in their images, we arrange the artifacts on the wall and on a table at the front of the room. In the center of that wall, we have already posted two large manila envelopes, one labeled "stereotypes" and the other "realities." Beside them is a large poster paper with two columns also labeled "stereotypes" and "realities." Once everything is assembled for all to view, we hand out index cards and give students five to ten minutes to look over the images and to think about what else they know or have heard about Indians and to write as many of these ideas as they can think of as one-sentence statements on their cards. Giving a basic example for each side helps students get started (e.g., "All Indians get free money from the government." / "Members of some tribes get various benefits from their own tribe's businesses and programs or rights linked to their treaty agreements with the federal government."). We usually choose to keep responses anonymous so students feel freer to generate ideas they are unsure about and raise assumptions they might feel uncomfortable discussing. There are very good arguments for holding students accountable for what they write (and ensuring that they all contribute), but at this early stage in the work we opt to take off a little pressure to make dealing with difficult issues a bit easier. We want students to get their ideas and assumptions out in the open because we cannot address misconceptions we aren't aware of. As students write down their ideas, they drop each into whichever envelope they think it belongs. After everyone is finished, the teacher takes one envelope, reads the statements, and asks the class if each is accurately placed as a stereotype or a reality. This allows us to move past duplicate statements and to skip, for now, irrelevant, offensive, or nonproductive statements such as those that are overtly racist without drawing undue attention to them. This is a useful precaution for pacing how much ignorance and controversy to take on at one time.

When the class comes to consensus on each statement, we tape the card under the appropriate column. If no consensus is reached, we post the idea to the side of the chart. We tell students that where we place ideas is not permanent, but throughout the unit we can continue to move the statements around as we learn more.

What students write will vary widely and will be influenced by everything from their age and academic background to their geographical location to the ethnic makeup of the class doing the exercise. Even doing this activity on an Indian reservation with classes of both white and Native students yields mixed results. Some classes are already aware of the many stereotypes of Native American people and can eloquently explain the realities. Other classes can become tense quickly because it's clear they know the "right" answer or what they are expected to say about stereotypes, but it's also clear that their personal experiences or family opinions make them want to speak to the stereotype. In other situations, some students genuinely have no experience with Indian culture (sometimes, surprisingly, even if they've lived on the reservation for years) but do have questions they've been afraid to ask. Regardless of the class makeup, the exercise is a good tool for giving you a basic idea of students' knowledge base.

After all the statements have been placed, each student chooses one from either the stereotype or the reality side to examine further for homework. The next time we meet, students report to the class what they learned and share at least two sources used to gather information. The range of ideas and information students report is generally wide. They might find facts that disprove statements or explanations for origins of some stereotypes, but it is also likely they will find information that supports stereotypes. Not all Indians gamble or earn huge incomes from reservation casinos, but there are some large casinos and a small percentage of tribal people in the United States do have sizable incomes from gaming. Not all Indians drink, but alcoholism is a significant problem on many reservations. As students share what they find, discussion should be carefully moderated to help students sort through what they have discovered and to prevent perpetuation of misconceptions.[2]

Viewing

To introduce *Smoke Signals* and keep students thinking about the issues we discussed in our previewing activities, we share two quotes from interviews with Alexie:

> I just try to write about everyday Indians, the kind of Indian I am who is just as influenced by the Brady Bunch as I am by my tribal traditions, who spends as much time going to the movies as I do going to ceremonies. (Mabrey par. 8)

> What's revolutionary or groundbreaking about the film is that the characters in it are Indians and they're fully realized hu-

man beings. They're not just the sidekick, or the buddy, they're the protagonists. Simply having Indians as the protagonists in a contemporary film and placing them within this familiar literary and cinematic structure is groundbreaking. (West and West par. 9)

Before watching the film, each student chooses a specific aspect of filmmaking to focus on while keeping in mind the question: How does this film play into or break down mainstream America stereotypes of Indians?

The different components of filmmaking students pay attention to are cinematic style, character development, music and sound, use of humor, and historical references.

Cinematic Style

Bringing a story to life in film requires more than strong text. What viewers see makes a huge impact on the viewing experience and ultimately on their opinion of the story. Directors and cinematographers put a lot of work into deciding what will fill the frame. Students evaluate how effectively they have done their jobs. Pay attention to:

- Camera movement: What is the camera angle (above action, below, straight on)? What is the distance of the camera from the action (far shot, medium shot, close-up, extreme close-up)?
- Framing/composition: What is included in each shot? What is left out? How is the main focus of the shot framed?
- Lighting: What is the source? Is it artificial or natural? What is the level of intensity? What direction is it coming from?
- Editing/montage (length of shots, rhythm, relationship of one shot to the next).
- Transitions (dissolve, fade-in/out, splicing) between scenes and

between the flashbacks (from past and present); splicing between two events happening simultaneously.

Alexie criticizes stereotypical Indian images in the movies like the brief flash of one of the main characters in *Powwow Highway* dressed in a full Indian warrior outfit with a tomahawk as he jumps into a fight, or one of the actors in *Thunderheart* turning into a deer (West and West par. 11–12). Though he found these movies more realistic than most in their portrayals of Indian people, he wanted to avoid this type of imagery and these sorts of transitions in *Smoke Signals*. Has he? He also says he is "rarely interested in traditional narrative" and has always been "fascinated with dreams and stories and flashing forward and flashing backward and playing with conventions of time" (West and West par. 26–27). He wants to include those elements, too. Is he successful?

As students view the film, we direct them to jot down three to four single shots or brief scenes that they like, to describe what is memorable about each (What's the frame? What is cut out? What's the camera angle? What is the lighting like?), and to tell why they think the shot or scene is effective. What impact does it have on the viewer's emotional reaction to the situation or the characters?

Character Development

Just as in written text, filmmakers pay attention to character development so the people in their stories seem real, distinctive, and memorable. According to Mabrey, Alexie wants "to shatter Hollywood's stereotypes of Indians as Tonto and the noble savage. 'That's so tiring. Who wants to be wise, you know? You get carpal tunnel syndrome from carrying the burden of your race,'

Alexie says. 'I'd like to have villains. I'd like to have goofballs.' Alexie says he tried to do this with his film *Smoke Signals*. 'One of the heroes was this geeky, androgynous, verbose, irritating Indian guy'" (qtd. in Mabrey par. 19–23).

We ask students to pay attention to the characters in this movie: "Are these the Indians described on the stereotypes list? If not, what strengths are portrayed by the characters on screen? What characteristics show up?" Students choose one of the main characters (Victor, Arnold, Thomas, or Suzy) and record details about at least three elements of characterization. They look for details of character traits and how they are conveyed. Possibilities to consider:

- Decisions and actions throughout the film
- Appearance: wardrobe/costume, hair, makeup
- Speech: content of dialogue, unique speech patterns, distinct phrases or words
- Personality quirks (like Thomas closing his eyes to tell stories)

After following a chosen character through the film, students decide if the character develops during the course of the film, whether the character's behavior seems motivated and consistent. They decide whether the character is realistic or caricatured and provide examples to back up their conclusions.

Music and Sound

Taken for granted by many viewers, a film's audio track (including both music and the background sounds) plays a huge role in creating the emotional and psychological impact of a film. Aware of how important the music would be to the movie, Alexie even wrote the lyrics to some of the songs and had specific ideas about which genre of music (rock vs. traditional) to include and when.

Some of the musical pieces have English words, western-style intervals and rhythms, as well as traditional Indian singing and drumming. Sounds of cars, wind, and fire might go undetected if they aren't pointed out to students.

We ask students to pay attention to these audio components of the film, to notice whether they are unique, and to describe the impact of the film's sound. Specifically, we ask students to pinpoint three to four specific times when the sound really seems to move the influence, direction, or tone of the story in either a positive or a negative way. Students may focus on song lyrics, music, background noises, voice-over dialogue, etc. For each sound moment chosen, they write a few sentences in which they discuss how the sound track supports or distracts from the story. Students consider whether the sound is surprising or anticipated and whether it reinforces stereotypes or offers something new.

Use of Humor

Alexie tries to break down stereotypes through humor: "I think humor is the most effective political tool out there, because people will listen to anything if they're laughing. . . . Humor is really just about questioning the status quo, that's all it is" (West and West par. 66). Students consider whether he pulls it off in *Smoke Signals*. We ask them to decide whether Alexie's humor allows him to guide audiences into considering important but tough issues by examining the following:

- As you watch, list in a two-column chart both examples of humor and examples of difficult issues from the Indian community that Alexie addresses in the film.
- After the movie ends, look at the lists you've compiled and write a paragraph in which you discuss how well you think Alexie has

balanced these two goals. Does he manage to be both humorous and address important, serious Native issues at the same time? Explain.

Historical References

Alexie is interested in expanding the version of mainstream western history to include Native American experiences and points of view. His writing and this film provide great materials to help students understand postcolonial ideas as they read and research. All his work is sprinkled with references to important tribal leaders from the past as well as major conflicts and battles. We want students to focus on those included in the film by completing the following activities:

- Keep a running list of references to significant people and events in Indian history. If you aren't sure, write it down and you can check after the film is over.
- Choose two of these references and explain how they are related to what is happening in the film. Why do you think Alexie thinks it is important to include references to the past if the film is taking place in modern times?

After viewing is completed and students have had time (in class or as homework) to write up the details they gathered and conclusions they've drawn while watching, we return once again to our initial question: How does this film play into or break down mainstream America stereotypes of Indians? We give everyone a few minutes to write to that prompt, reminding them to pull details from their viewing to support their ideas, and then we use that work to begin class discussion.

Wrapping Up: Reexamining Indian Roles in the Story of America

To pull our concluding discussion back to the film, students rewatch Chapter 11 and part of 12. (The entire clip from the beginning until the bus pulls into Phoenix is about 5:45 minutes.) We direct students' attention to two issues (possibly dividing the class in half and assigning one to each section):

- "Real Indians"
  What advice does Victor give Thomas? What does he tell him a real Indian is like? Victor slips into a mini-monologue in which he tells Thomas that his current look isn't cutting it. His advice ranges from "you got to be mean if you want any respect" to "an Indian man ain't nothin' without his hair." Make a list of everything Victor tells Thomas about being an Indian. Why is it important to be a "real" Indian? What does this seem to imply (or directly state) about the consequences of not fulfilling the stereotype?

- "Cowboys Always Win"
  Throughout this scene, Thomas keeps repeating that "the cowboys always win." How does the conflict in this scene echo or make fun of some of those cowboy–Indian conflicts from other films? Is this scene a modern-day take on the cowboy–Indian conflict? Why or why not?

After we discuss these specific scenes, we think again about the focus point (what a "real Indian" is like or that "cowboys always win") and generalize to the movie as a whole. We use these questions to generate discussion: "What does this movie really show us about real Indians?" "How do the characters we meet compare with the list Victor gives?" "How does this movie compare with others with Indian characters?" "Do the Indians lose yet again here? Why or why not?"

Postviewing Extension

For students to really understand *Smoke Signals* and what Alexie accomplishes, it is helpful for them to look at the ways Indians have been portrayed in other movies. We divide students into groups (about three to five works best). Each group chooses a film to watch together (or on their own schedule and discuss together) in which Indians play a significant role. We pull some possibilities from films Alexie has talked about in interviews or referenced in his creative work, including *The Searchers* (1956), *Powwow Highway* (1989), the Lone Ranger and Tonto movies (a number of titles available), *Thunderheart* (1992), *Little Big Man* (1970), any number of John Wayne films, *The Business of Fancydancing* (2002), *Dances with Wolves* (1990), or *The Last of the Mohicans* (1992). Other possibilities might include *One Flew Over the Cuckoo's Nest* (1975), *War Party* (1988), *Clearcut* (1991), *Black Robe* (1991), *Geronimo* (1993), *Cheyenne Warrior* (1994), *Skins* (2002), or even Disney's *Pocahontas* (1995). These films have various ratings and like any materials will not all be suitable for all audiences, but all offer much to talk about in terms of Indian portrayals. Many students will also have suggestions of their own.

After choosing a film, students are given the following tasks to complete over the span of two to three class periods:

1. Watch the film, paying attention to the Indian characters portrayed.
2. Write a one-page written response and evaluation. Explain what you liked and thought was well done in the film as well as what you found unimpressive. To help organize your paper, choose

two to three of the elements the class focused on while viewing *Smoke Signals* (cinematic style, character development, music and sound, use of humor, historical references) to comment on and also include one section about which you decide if you could make an argument for the film as a postcolonial text. Bring this to class and be ready to turn it in after using it to guide your discussion with others who watched the same film.

3. After discussing your initial impression of the film with your group, everyone needs to find a different critical review of the film and write a second one-page response paper. Compare the reviewer's ideas with your own, offering at least two specific passages from the film (different from those the reviewer uses) to support your points. Again, bring this to class and be ready to turn it in after using it to guide your group's discussion.

4. Work with your group, giving each member a chance to summarize and share highlights from the review he or she read, emphasizing where you agreed and disagreed with the reviewer.

5. Prepare a group presentation that teaches the rest of the class about the film you've been discussing. Make sure you have all the following components:

   ■ Overview of film: title, year, director, one- to three-sentence plot summary

   ■ Professional reviewers' opinions, including one to two very brief quotes from the reviews you read that give the class a good idea of the overall tone of the reviews

   ■ Your group's opinions of the film and thoughts on its portrayal of Indians

   ■ Your group's decision on whether the film can be interpreted as a postcolonial text

   ■ Five-minute (maximum) clip from the actual film with explanation of why the group chose the excerpt and what they think it illustrates

After each group has presented, we debrief by reading Alexie's poem "How to Write the Great American Indian Novel" from *The Summer of Black Widows*. We give each student a copy of the poem and ask them to read it completely through once. Then we have them read it again and decide on one sentence that summarizes the poem's message and one word that describes the poem's tone. Students share their selections and we discuss what Alexie might want readers to think about, realize, or reconsider as they read this poem.

Next, we put a copy of the poem on an overhead and ask students to find as many lines as they can that describe events from any of the movies they watched (*Smoke Signals*, the ones they just presented on, or others they have seen independently in the past) and explain any connections. We underline the lines from the poem they connect with movies. We finish with a reflective writing prompt:

Do you think stereotypes about Indians show up in film? What are they? How does Alexie's film compare with others you have viewed and discussed? Are his portrayals similar or different? How so? Where does he seem to pay homage to these other films? How does he poke fun at them? Reference any specific lines, images, or scenes. Describe any trends in ways Indians are portrayed on screen over time. What evidence of postcolonialism did you find in the films you watched?

Multimodal Extensions

Like Alexie, many of our students already are (albeit amateur) producers of these kinds of texts. It behooves us to develop activities to help our students write more technology-informed, visual arguments such as inviting them to use features of PowerPoint to construct persuasive visual arguments (beyond the typical ho-hum repetitive delivery organized by the Microsoft PowerPoint wizard); to use iMovie or Movie Maker to edit video clips from the presentations with their own video captures into powerful persuasive visual arguments; or to use Dreamweaver software to produce Web-based articulations of what they have learned in complex, multimodal, multimedia texts. Although some of us worry that the new media are imperiling our students' attention spans, writing skills, and so forth, it is vital in the twenty-first century to celebrate technologies that borrow from the visual artist's instinct for pattern, contrast, unity, and balance and from the poet's ability to posit, to juxtapose, and to condense, as has Alexie with *Smoke Signals*. Doing so enables us and our students to learn to compose using a new and proliferating writing technology in which students are already dabbling and that allows them to write intertextual and hypertextual responses to curricular content developed in striking visual formats. By experimenting with image and sound, students can compose dramatic portrayals that speak strongly about issues of significance to them. Not to do so means to watch as they leave us behind.

Conclusion

Working with *Smoke Signals* helps students both explore how Native people have been portrayed and think about the authenticity of stories. Alexie chose the title *Smoke Signals* for this film because it conjures stereotypical images of Indians sending smoke signals across the plains with blankets, an image regularly portrayed in the comic strip *Mother Goose and Grimm*, but it also fit the theme of fire that runs through the film. Alexie comments, "in a contemporary sense, smoke signals are about calls of distress, calls for help. That's really what this movie is all about" (West and West par. 37). Ultimately, this film sends a powerful signal to viewers that there is more to Indian people than past movies have shown. Movies are, as Oliver Stone has called them, "first drafts." They are not the complete explanation for anything or the final judgment we leave on an issue, but "they raise questions and inspire students to find out more" (Carnes 306). Viewing *Smoke Signals* helps students begin that inquiry and think more deeply about the power of visual representation to influence understanding.

Notes

1. Students can view images posted in the archives of The American Indian College Fund at http://www.collegefund.org/news/ad_sari.html. The archives house a series of "Have You Ever Seen a Real Indian?" print ads that ran from 2001 through 2006 featuring accomplished American Indian professionals and tribal college students as a way to portray a contemporary and accurate image of Native American people.

2. Devon Mihesuah's *American Indians: Stereotypes and Realities* is an excellent resource for this activity. Mihesuah is Choctaw and a history professor at Northern Arizona University. The book addresses twenty-four common misconceptions about American Indians. The text is accessible to students; more important, however, teachers with little background in Native issues will find it incredibly helpful to read this book before trying to implement this activity in the classroom.

3 The Lone Ranger and Tonto Fistfight in Heaven: Alexie and History

■■■■■■■■■■■■■■■■■■■■■■■■■■■■■■■■■■■■

The Lone Ranger and Tonto Fistfight in Heaven, Sherman Alexie's first collection of short stories, published in 1993 and reissued with an introduction and two new stories in 2005, takes place primarily on the Spokane Indian Reservation and features several peripatetic characters who shift and morph through the stories, giving the collection a novel-like impression. Reading the collection can be challenging on many levels. One challenge derives from this morphing of characters and the nonchronological organization of time. Other challenges arise because the characters discuss tough issues, the language is uncensored, the lifestyles portrayed are at times depressing and filled with dangerous and unhealthy behavior, and the historical events the characters talk about and live with are unpleasant. Though these characteristics can make a teacher's job difficult, they also lend the volume, at least partially, its strength. *Partially.* Alexie is also an incredible storyteller. His writing is poetic and humorous, and *LRTFIH* is one of the more accessible books for acquainting students with American Indian history and reservation life.

Because Alexie writes about some of the sensitive social and economic troubles that plague Indian people, his work has been called "ambiguous in its implications for Native American struggle" (Dix 158). Critics (both Indian and white) have accused him of pandering to white expectations and merely portraying stereotypes. In the book, one of Alexie's storytelling characters is given the advice: "You should write a story about something good, a real good story. . . . [P]eople should know that good things always happen to Indians, too" (*LRTFIH* 140). It's probably safe to assume that at least one person has given Alexie similar advice.

While Alexie does use the reservation and all its problems as a backdrop for his stories, he is doing more than giving readers what they want and expect—those stereotypical and cliché Indians. However, we need to help students through the process of interacting with the text and help them see that his characters are not "self-destructive losers" but "sympathetic, complex individuals trying to cope within a racist society" (Coulombe 99), to see that the stories "delineate not only the harsh cultural realities facing Indians (both on and off the reservation) but also the pride and strength that sustain them" (105). The ongoing debate about the implications of Alexie's work makes it a great text for introducing students to primary concepts in critical race theory and helping them to develop some familiarity with historical and contemporary Native American issues. It is a text that is rich with possibilities.

"Every Little Hurricane"

The first story in *LRTFIH* works well not only as an introduction to the collection but also as an introduction to reservation life, with all its challenges, histories, and cultural influences. Before giving students the book or this specific story, we ask them to write for a few minutes on what they think a story titled "Every Little Hurricane" might be about. Next, we tell them that Alexie is using the idea of hurricanes as a metaphor, and to think about what the storm might represent as they read. The metaphor is obvious, so students can identify pretty easily what Alexie is doing. After we have talked about that as a group, students look at the story again, this time pulling out all the "hurricanes" or "little storms" that Victor and his family and friends endure.

We then assemble a list of all these "storms." Compiling the list serves as both introduction and warning. It lets students know what kinds of issues these stories take on and previews what they can expect as we move into the text. This first story is also a relatively safe way to begin looking at how race influences events and personal interactions, and it provides a smooth segue into researching some of the unfamiliar historical and cultural references readers will encounter.

American Indian History: Introductory Research

After introducing *LRTFIH* but before reading too far, it is helpful to have students research some of the historical events that are referenced throughout the collection. All of Alexie's works expect his readers to know some things about American Indian history. Though his storytelling is strong enough for most stories to make sense and be engaging even if readers have no background in Indian history, even a superficial level of awareness of the cultural and historical events and people he sprinkles throughout his stories will give students a much deeper understanding. Although no substitute for in-depth research on a topic, even a one-class, mini-research session followed by a class in which students present what they have learned can significantly move forward students' understanding. Anyone can gain preliminary knowledge of some of these topics by doing a quick Internet search. It is an easy way to start, useful for gathering a lot of information quickly, and a great way to introduce or reinforce some lessons on the authenticity and authority of Internet sites. Checking information sources when investigating American Indian history is especially critical because so much misinformation exists. Information posted by tribal or state governments is likely to be more authentic and accurate than information posted elsewhere. We always look first for evidence of tribal affiliation and enrollment of writers or for work compiled by Native American educators or Native studies scholars. Oyate is an organization devoted to authenticating educational materials and texts for use in classrooms (see http://www.oyate.org).

As students choose a topic to research, they simultaneously build critical literacy skills and background knowledge in Indian history. This initial foray into research also exposes students to a variety of issues that for many of them may be new and gets them thinking about which topics they might be interested in exploring in more depth for a larger research project after reading the text.

Possible research topics referenced by Alexie in these short stories and elsewhere in his work include:

- Broken Native American treaties
- Crazy Horse
- Coeur d'Alene /Schitsu' Umsh tribe
- Commodity food
- General George Armstrong Custer
- Coerced sterilization of Native American women
- Coeur d'Alene War/Spokane Plains War
- Colonel Wright and 1858 horse slaughter (see Figure 3.1, p. 43)
- Chief Til-co-ax
- Ghost Dance (Alexie's quote from Wovoka is a good starting point)
- HUD Houses (U.S. Department of Housing and Urban Development)

- Indian Health Service/tribal hospitals
- Dawes Act/allotment of Native lands
- Smallpox-infected blankets
- Diabetes in Native American populations
- Sacred Black Hills/Mount Rushmore
- Stick game
- Spokane Indian Reservation
- Owl Dance
- Fancydancing
- Uranium mining on Native American land
- Massacre at Wounded Knee

As students research, they should gather enough information to create a one-page, single-sided handout for the class that summarizes what they have learned. We ask our students to include the following:

- Title/research topic
- 200–300-word summary of what they learned
- A brief, interesting, and relevant quote from one of their sources
- A three- to five-item bulleted list of important facts, or a timeline of four to five important dates
- At least one image or diagram
- At least three complete citations of resources

Students always ask to extend the one-page rule, but we stick to it firmly. A great deal of information can fit on one page if students pay attention to formatting. Selection and condensation of information as well as thoughtful presentation are important multimodal strategies to master; we want students to focus on what is most important and how to arrange it effectively. We include organization and aesthetics in evaluation of the final piece to emphasize their importance.

The Horse Slaughter of 1858

In the spring of 1858 Colonel Steptoe of the U.S. army left the safety of Fort Walla Walla. The Colonel was going to a peaceful meeting with the Native Tribes from the Colville area. Unbeknownst to him and his soldiers, they  were being followed. What ensued was a terrible defeat for the army. After the long hot summer, Colonel George Wright went back with about 700 soldiers and 30 NezPerce scouts to avenge Colonel Steptoe's defeat. These men not only had the advantage of firepower, but also superior numbers. When the soldiers reached Four Lakes they engaged the Coeur d'Alene, Palouse, and Spokan Indians. Unfortunately for the Indians they were overconfident and rode straight at the soldiers suffering heavy losses. The Indians retreated and lost the small battle. After resting for a few days Colonel Wright continued up the Spokan Valley to pursue the Indians. He burned anything that the Indians left behind. On September 9 the soldiers found a group of horses near what is now called Liberty Lake. He decided to slaughter the horses to prevent the natives from using them. Throughout the day and most of the next the soldiers shot all but 100 of the horses to be used for the troops. But these untrained mounts were useless and it was decided to shoot them as well. This area became known as Horse Slaughter Camp, and is near the present day town of Aturdee, Washington. The slaughtering of the horses was a crippling blow to the natives as they were vital to the Indians survival, and large numbers of the old and young died from starvation that winter.

- May 6 1858—Colonel Steptoe defeated by native tribes
- Sep. 1 1858—Colonel Wright engaged natives at the Battle of Four Lakes
- Sep. 9 1858—Slaughter of 800 horses near Liberty Lake

"A blow has been struck that they will never forget" —Colonel Steptoe

Lutey, Tom. "Marker Recalls 1858 Slaughter of Horses." 10 Jan 2008 <http:// www. spokesmanreview.com/local/story.asp?ID=176313>
"U.S. Army Colonel George Wright Slaughters 800 Palouse Horses on September 8, 1858." 10 Jan. 2008 <http://www.historylink.org/essays/ output.cfm? file_id=5142>
"Colonel George Wright and Indian Wars." 10 Jan 2008 <http://www.discovery-school.org/1504108931827540/blank/browse.asp?a=383&BMDRN=2000& BCOB=0&c=5400>

Figure 3.1. Student sample research handout.

Once students have formatted their work, they make copies so that everyone in the class has a handout. In some cases, students can simply create an overhead of the document to refer to as they share what they have learned. The advantage of each student having hard copies, however, is that they can refer to them as they continue reading *LRTFIH*. When they come to an unfamiliar concept in Alexie's text, they can look back at their classmates' handouts to refresh their memories.

After students have had a day to collect and assemble information, we take another day to share what we have learned. To keep class moving quickly, each student gets only two to three minutes to highlight the most interesting or important concepts. If classmates want to know more, discussion about those issues can continue in subsequent classes. This also helps students realize how much more they have to learn and helps them to decide what else they might want to research.

Thematic Exploration: Recurring Themes and Topics

Alexie addresses many difficult issues in *LRTFIH*, so much so that students sometimes decide that his stories are just about Indian problems. Many curriculum guides for reading Native American literature suggest that students extend understanding by examining contemporary problems common in Indian country. We do not recommend the approach, because too often these exercises reinforce stereotypes rather than break them down. While the stories in *LRTFIH* necessitate discussion of the problems they bring up, students' understanding of Native American issues is better served by having students spend time researching history and resultant policies and analyzing what role race plays in our understanding of the issues, rather than gathering support for negative assumptions they may already hold.

Another more productive option is to challenge students to investigate a problem raised by Alexie and find a specific example or story of a reservation or individual Native who is defying that stereotype. Alexie himself provides a living example. Readily accessible resources include the website for the American Indian College Fund (http://www.collegefund.org/scholarships/main.html), radio broadcasts and the website for National Native News (http://www.nativenews.net/), *Indian Country Today* (The Nations' Leading American Indian News Source) (http://www.indiancountry.com), and the website Indianz.com (http://www.indianz.com).

Instead of having them examine problems, we direct each student to choose a topic from a list of suggested possibilities to track and study while reading the stories in the collection. Multiple students can track the same topic, but individually they keep a reading response log in which, as they read, they identify and summarize places in the text where their topic shows up, recording page numbers, direct quotes of powerful lines, and any personal reactions or questions they have regarding their selected topic. In the following list, we summarize some possible topics. This list and the explanations included can be used as background or introductory guide for teachers or as a tool to help focus students.

■ Resiliency
   Many of the characters in *LRTFIH* are up against some difficult things, but they are survivors. "All I Wanted to Do Was Dance" chronicles one difficult situation after the next for alcoholic Victor, but the story ends with optimism:

> And they laughed. And Victor kept laughing as he walked. And
> he was walking down this road and tomorrow maybe he would
> be walking down another road and maybe tomorrow he would
> be dancing. Victor might be dancing.

Yes, Victor would be dancing. (92)

How do these characters cope? What helps them go on when they have battles of all kinds to fight every day? Alexie shows us how his characters gather strength in every story. Imagination is key for some. There is Victor's mom, whose "medicine and magic" (5) help the family survive every hard time. Victor's dad advises him to "[r]emember what happened immediately before" (34) rather than remembering the bad things. Additionally, the stories are populated with characters who pull strength from music and dancing of all kinds.

- Community
  Many of the stories emphasize the importance of extended family and community. At one point, the narrator explains, "I know some- body must be thinking about us because if they didn't we'd just disappear" (119). Characters' relationships with others keep them alive. A sense of connectedness and interdependence between the people in the stories resonates in both big and small ways. Norma explains at one point, "Every one of our elders who dies takes a piece of our past away. . . . And that hurts more because I don't know how much of a future we have" (167). The people around them link characters to the past, to their hopes for the future, and to what makes the present enjoyable or at least endurable. Norma tells Junior that Indians "don't just watch things happen. Watch- ing automatically makes the watcher part of the happening." Be- cause of this, "everything matters. Even the little things" (200). Character well-being is connected to that of those around them.

- Storytelling: Power of Language and Words
  LRTFIH provides a partial argument for storytelling as a means of survival. Characters in nearly every story tell stories, remember stories, or emphasize the power of language and stories to change

their lives. Victor's father even offers him stories as an "apology" (26). Much of this emphasis on storytelling is embodied in Thomas Builds-the-Fire (who once "held the reservation postmaster hostage for eight hours with the idea of a gun" [93]) and who, like his grandfather and great-grandfather, both Samuel Builds-the-Fire, had "the gift of storytelling" and "could pick up the pieces of a story from the street and change the world for a few moments" (132). Many characters share belief in the strength of storytelling, but there is also awareness that what one says can be destructive as well as helpful. Victor says that "arguments were just as damaging as a fist. Words can be like that, you know?" (185). He also questions, "How can we imagine a new language when the language of the enemy keeps our dismembered tongues tied to his belt. How can we imagine a new alphabet when the old jumps off billboards down into our stomachs?" (152). Even in this despair, there is awareness that whoever controls language controls many aspects of society as well. Samuel

> knew his stories had the power to teach, to show how this life should be lived. He would often tell his children and their friends, and then their grandchildren and their friends, those stories which could make their worlds into something better. At the very least, he could tell funny stories that would make each day less painful. (134)

Story is used throughout the book to teach, redeem, transform, and heal.

■ Warriors

Alexie has often commented that he wants to expand readers' notions of what Native people are like beyond the common image of the stereotypical Indian warrior; still, he has not moved away from the warrior theme. Many of his characters look for ways to still be warriors, and yet they feel as though there is nowhere left to prove themselves in the same way their warrior ancestors did. Thomas tells about

> these two little Indian boys who wanted to be warriors. But it was too late to be warriors in the old way. All the horses were gone. So the two Indian boys stole a car and drove into the city. They parked the stolen car in front of the police station and then hitchhiked back to the reservation. (63)

Alexie's characters complain that they have no actual wars to fight (29) and show "little warriors looking for some honor in twentieth-century vandalism" (44).

Alexie develops many contemporary warriors, who include basketball warriors with "twentieth-century horses we called our legs" (118). There is also Dirty Joe, whose flat face is "a map of all the wars he fought in the Indian bars. Dirty Joe was no warrior in the old sense" (54). Junior Polatkin knows that people think he "was supposed to make it, to rise above the rest of the reservation . . . the new kind of warrior" (188). Again and again we are reminded that these characters are trying to find ways to show they are ready for battles of all kinds.

■ Music

Music is a central character in many of the stories. At times we hear traditional singing and drumming, but Jimi Hendrix and Hank Williams are just as resonant. When Victor's father is in the hospital after a motorcycle wreck, his mother "sang Indian tunes under her breath, in time with the machines" hooked up to his father (33). Still, Victor tells us it is Robert Johnson who really "understood what it meant to be Indian on the edge of the twenty-first century, even if he was black at the beginning of the twentieth." Many stories in the collection use many different kinds of music to make the case that "music had powerful medicine" (29).

■ Basketball

Basketball, possibly more than any other activity, makes its way into these stories. Alexie writes, "a reservation hero is a hero forever. In fact, their status grows over the years as the stories are told and retold" (48). The reservation community starts scouting players early (in one story, they talk about "a little warrior," Lucy, only a third grader, but already a promising ball player). Because basketball is so important, "it hurts to lose any of them [talented players] because Indians see ball players as saviors" (52). The basketball court is the new battlefield where young people prove themselves and heroes are made. Julius Windmaker was "the latest in a long line of reservation basketball heroes, going all the way back to Aristotle Polatkin, who was shooting jumpshots exactly one year before James Naismith supposedly invented basketball" (45). In this collection, most of Alexie's heroes have proved themselves on the basketball court.

■ Dancing

Like music and basketball, dancing is key to many aspects of the characters' lives. Dancing offers protection, tradition, change, power, and entertainment and fills many other voids. There are references to cultural dances—traditional, fancy, owl—throughout the collection, but just as often characters dance contemporary dances. Characters talk about the Ghost Dance and its power to rid them of white people and the problems that arrived with them. Victor fancydances in the same outfit his father wore when he was eight or nine years old, but as an adult Victor describes dancing as "his compensation, his confession, largest sin and penance" (83). Norma "had given dance lessons at the Arthur Murray Dance Studio to pay her way through community college. She also danced topless in a Seattle bar to put food in her child's stomach" (78). When desperate, knowing something in her life needs to shift, Norma puts on a beaded dress so heavy no one has ever been able to wear it and begins to dance: "Dancing that way, she knew things were beginning to change" (82).

As students track topics, they see that many overlap. For example, community often centers on basketball, and, at times, basketball players are respected as modern-day warriors. Most all of these topics can be linked to others. Helping students see these connections begins to give them a picture of what the place Alexie writes about looks and feels like.

Because students focus on a particular thematic aspect of the collection from beginning to end, by the time they've finished the text they're prepared with the textual support they need to complete an expository writing assignment. With this approach, students also take responsibility for class discussion. Every day at least a few students are chosen to initiate discussion by sharing examples from the book that illustrate aspects of the theme they are tracking. We talk about the class's questions or ideas about the theme. Different mixes of students have more responsibility for talking on different days because themes ebb and flow through the stories. To turn our exploration into a group effort, we make posters for each topic to post around the room where students can trace various concepts by continuously adding events, quotes, questions, etc., as the class moves through the book. To extend this activity, students can find one other piece of Alexie's writing (short story, poem, essay, film, novel, song) that deals with the topic each is exploring. Much of Alexie's work is guided by similar themes.

After students have tracked one idea throughout the collection, they are armed with both the confidence and the content to create a strong persuasive essay or critical review of the book. We use some of the professional models excerpted in Chapter 6 as examples. Although creating an argument about literature and defending it is a difficult task at any level, the high-level thinking and organizational skills involved in writing a critical essay are more manageable when students come to the assignment with some ideas and opinions of their own and some textual references with which to work.

Finding a theme or an argument within the material students have gathered is much easier than trying to do so from the book as a whole. As students read and generate examples, they prepare to construct an argument about a theme they see emerging and to make a case about what they think Alexie is doing in his writing. We are better able to guide students to develop an argument as we look at their collections of notes and references because we see evidence of their interests and opinions. We tailor the amount of guidance we give students based on their needs. When a more personal option seems desirable, students can compose a comparison essay in which they identify a theme from Alexie's book and discuss the similarities and differences between events or characters in *LRTFIH* and events or people in their own community.

Writing from Models: "Indian Education"

Alexie's poetry and prose share many stylistic similarities. In either genre, his writing is both narrative and poetic. This combination appeals to high school students, makes his writing accessible, and provides models that students can work with to learn aspects of Alexie's craft. Mimicking his sense of organization, rhythm, and style and incorporating them in their own writing can help students develop their writing skills and arrange their content. One story in *LRTFIH* that works especially well for modeling this is "Indian Education." The title conveys two meanings simultaneously; it is a story about one Indian's school experiences as well as about the processes of becoming educated in what it means to be an Indian in our society.

Though the story is clear and easy to understand, race is central to the narrator's experiences; from his point of view, his being Indian is the characteristic that most determines his educational experience. Some students will be resistant to reading something that doesn't paint white people in a favorable light or that at times seems to group them together as the same generic, unappealing persona. After reading the story, Annela commented, "He paints all whites as dim-witted apathetic fascists. This is unfair. I know it's irony and he's only trying to construct an interesting way to tell his story, but sometimes it can be offensive." Reactions like Annela's are typical and valid. They are also a great opening to introduce students to critical race theory.

The uncomfortable position Alexie's work put Annela in might be new to many students, but her feelings might resonate with nonwhite students (or their teachers) who have struggled through texts whose only minority characters show up as flat or stereotypical caricatures. After reading "Indian Education" and the criticism, Melinda had the opposite reaction. Alexie's narrator seemed familiar: "I relate to Alexie's work," she shared, "but others, . . . white and other ethnic groups not familiar with reservation Natives[,] would not relate to the true meaning of his work. A lot of his work seems to be like an inside joke. It's interesting to hear people say that they don't like his work because they don't understand." It's important to discuss with students all the different reactions they have to a text like Alexie's. Though initially it may seem counterintuitive, often talking about racial issues isn't a distraction from looking at the writing craft; instead, getting that aspect of the work out in the open can facilitate a more useful discussion of the craft. For Alexie and many other writers, probably even some of our students, race is not separate from stylistic aspects—it's intertwined.

In most situations in contemporary society, the "colorblind" approach is considered the most acceptable way to deal (or essentially not deal) with issues of race. Most races can't clearly be defined in any scientific, cultural, or political[1] way, and it is not socially acceptable to point out racial differences. Students are often taught that they shouldn't see race, that race doesn't really matter, and that their own ethnic background shouldn't have any influence on how they look at a text. But students know that all this does matter. Even if they can't define it, race exists and is an important aspect of identity. This contradiction makes students resistant to discussing texts in which race is prominent.

If we want students to look at text critically, we need to equip them with, and then allow them to use, tools to discuss race:

> In the end, attention to differences is what interpretation is all about. Interpreting texts in the broadest sense . . . is not an attempt to erase difference. Rather such attention is an attempt to highlight the complexities that the social world puts before us—as we work to understand and respond to events, practices, beliefs, institutions, and various cultural artifacts. (Nealon and Giroux 163)

Students don't want to say something wrong or point out differences they've been taught are racist to notice. When students have no background in or familiarity with discussing issues of race, however, it's more likely their reactions *will* be racist because of their levels of ignorance. Pairing the reading of "Indian Education" with some of the critical pieces in Chapter 6 is a useful way to work through these issues. After working with the criticism, Annela discovered, "It helped me understand why Alexie writes the way he does." Melinda liked reading the critical reviews too, even though she didn't agree with them. Rather than ignoring issues of race, opening them up for discussion better equips students to navigate situations that involve race, both in texts and beyond them.

After reading and responding to the short story, we introduce the writing assignment by watching Chapter 11, "How to Be an Indian," from *Smoke Signals*. (The entire clip from the beginning until Thomas gets back on the bus is less than two minutes.) As we watch, students write down all the advice Victor gives Thomas about how to be a "real Indian." Once the clip is over, we share the advice and create a group list of the information we have collected. Victor tells Thomas what he thinks Thomas will need to do, and what people are expecting him to do, if he wants people to take him seriously as an Indian. After we finish discussing Victor's how-to guide for being an Indian, we brainstorm things we might write in our own how-to guides: "What roles might we tell others how to fulfill?" With this question in mind, we ask students to consider the following: "Have you ever felt others had certain expectations about how you should act, talk, or dress? Maybe it's because of the color of your skin, the language you speak, the neighborhood you live in, your family's religious practices, the friends you choose, or even the hobbies you have. Are there expected behaviors and beliefs that go along with these identities?" After coming up with possible examples, students write lists of all the different identities they have, whether they have ·· chosen them or someone else has assigned them. We use the guiding questions "How do you label yourself? How do others label you?" Examples we provide include labels such as "teenager," "Hispanic," "artist," "grandson," "athlete," etc. To get ideas flowing, we model by writing a list of our own identities on the board or overhead.

Once students have generated a small list, we ask them to pick one identity to write more about. We challenge them to come up with at least ten characteristics or expected behaviors or practices of that identity so they have some material from which to write. The lists students compose very often, with little revision, become powerful list poems. Students can take the assignment in many different directions:

How to Be a Teenage Boy

Text as often as possible.
Don't listen.
Make fun of everybody.
Make teachers lose it.
Be as dirty as possible.
Switch girlfriends like underwear.
Be innocent around parents, but the real you around friends.
Eat faster than you should.
Make inappropriate comments.
Drive 90 mph everywhere.
Make your life revolve around sports.

—Cubby

How to Be a French Daughter

Learn to listen.
Act/be snobby.
Learn to shop at the right places.
Have a bigger tolerance for lectures.
Speak with "zhe" accent.
Learn how to fill big shoes.

Desire to travel anywhere/everywhere.
Be respectful always.
Never assume you're correct when contradicting.
Be comfortable in high heels.
Accept quirky French habits.
Always be polite.
Know how to spell "quiche."

—Clare

Many students will have a nice piece of writing from this step, but we push them a bit further and ask them to try to think of some specific event (or multiple events if they can) that caused them to believe in each listed expectation. Then students choose at least five events and write them in narrative form. Following Alexie's lead in "Indian Education," students do not need to write the complete story for each event, because each segment is a snapshot of one moment in time. We dissect Alexie's model using craft analyses, described by both Katie Wood Ray in *Wondrous Words* and Randy Bomer in *Time for Meaning*, to highlight important techniques Alexie draws on to construct his snapshots of Indian education—dialogue, sensory description, setting, characterization, action. Students do not necessarily use all of these in every snapshot they write but generally focus on doing just one or two well.

Once students have gathered content, they choose an organizational structure that supports what they want to say in the piece. Alexie organizes his snapshots by grade level, which makes sense if the writing takes place in school. To help students decide what might work best in their writing, we pair them up and ask them to brainstorm as many organizational structures as they can. Other chronological options such as age or year arise in brainstorming sessions, but students also choose to arrange based on geographical location or on interactions with different people. Sometimes we set a short time limit (three to four minutes) and make it a contest between groups to see who can generate the most possibilities and help students decide how to organize and title each section of their writing. We also remind them to pay attention to three other organizational strategies: Does the overall title reflect the content or the main theme of your story? Does the first snapshot introduce your main theme? Does your last section conclude the writing? We caution students not to add any happily-ever-after, wrap-everything-up summaries, but to think about how to leave readers with an image, an idea, or a question, as Alexie does.

If time allows, students pair up and offer feedback and suggestions about the three organizational areas and/or elements of fiction they should have tried to incorporate in each section. After students have had time to polish those aspects of their writing, for the next revision exercise students return to Alexie for guidance. They reread "Indian Education" to look for examples of poetic devices.

Nearly every snapshot includes a range of poetic techniques. Before students begin rereading, we refresh their memories by asking them to explain any poetic devices they can remember and give an example from the story. We help them by pointing out such things as the simile describing how Alexie's character bloodies a kid so he "almost looked like he was wearing warpaint." Alexie incorporates hyperbole when, after the speaker kisses a white girl and tells her his name, "no one talks to him for another 500 years" and "he felt the goodbyes he was saying to his entire tribe." Personification and innuendo are at work in Alexie's description of the two hundred quilts his mother started one year and never finished that "sat in separate, dark places in our HUD house and wept savagely." He even uses clichéd figures of speech (like "tasting failure") and makes them less so through specificity, as when he describes the local people who "taste the failure in the tap water." We write our collective examples on the board or overhead so students have a reference when they reread.

Once students identify Alexie's use of poetic techniques and the class has shared what they've found, students return to their own drafts to see if they have used any of the same devices. If some have, we ask volunteers to share. Then the whole class takes up the task of adding at least two or three examples of poetic language to their stories. When students have finished, they have spent a lot of time with Alexie's story, discussing craft and the social issues he raises. They have also spent a substantial amount of time thinking about their own identities and working on several different aspects of their writing. This activity can be retooled so that students come up with a final piece that is either memoir or fiction. As described, this is a memoir exercise, but it isn't crucial that students write about actual events. Like any good fiction writer, students will probably write about events drawn from their lives, but these events do not need to be ones students have experienced. They could be events that students have witnessed or heard retold by others. While students needn't write about their own experiences, they should write what they know. In the words of one of Alexie's characters, "if it's fiction, then it better be true."[2]

Final Reflective Writing/Discussion

To wrap up our work with the story collection, we watch a short clip of one of the old Lone Ranger and Tonto movies or TV shows. Then we read the following passage from the story "The Only Traffic Signal on the Reservation Doesn't Flash Red Anymore":

> It's hard to be optimistic on the reservation. When a glass sits on the table here, people don't wonder if it's half filled or half

empty, they just hope it's good beer. Still, Indians have a way of surviving. But it's almost like Indians can easily survive the big stuff. Mass murder, loss of language and land rights. It's the small things that hurt the most. The white waitress who wouldn't take an order, Tonto, the Washington Redskins. (49)

Next, we take ten minutes to think about how the film clip and quote connect to the title of the book and to the title of the first story in the collection, "Every Little Hurricane," that we read to begin this unit. Then we reflect on the following questions:

- Why do you think Alexie chose those titles? What do you think he wants you to think about when you read them?
- Has either title taken on any new significance now that you've read the rest of the text and completed your research? Do the titles bring to mind something different than they did before you read the book? If so, what is different?
- How do you think your own race influenced your reaction to these stories? Did it make them more or less interesting? More or less relevant? In what other ways might race have influenced your reading? What leads you to think this?
- How important is the characters' race to these stories? If all the characters were white, would your opinion of the stories change? Would white characters change the realism? Why or why not?
- In the title, Alexie has the Lone Ranger and Tonto fighting. In what ways do Alexie's characters fight back in these stories? What are they doing to survive "every little hurricane"?
- What have you thought about these stories? About the book as a whole?

After reading this collection of stories, we might discuss the twenty-five-year effort to pass the United Nations Declaration on the Rights of Indigenous Peoples (September 2007) and the fact that the U.S. government voted against it.

Notes

1. Unlike other ethnic groups, Native Americans do have the unique distinction of being recognized by the U.S. government, and their tribal affiliation is not only cultural but also in part a political designation.

2. Other good pieces for modeling include "Every Little Hurricane" for extended metaphor and the "First Annual All-Indian Horseshoe Pitch and Barbecue" for use of repetition. Students can also emulate the structures of many Alexie poems, including "Family Cookbook," "A Reservation Table of the Elements," and "Reservation Mathematics," all from *First Indian on the Moon*, substituting their own details.

4 Slam! Writing and Performing Poetry

■ ■

Because Sherman Alexie is a four-time spoken-word poetry bout heavyweight world champion,[1] we provide guidance for using spoken-word performance poetry and slam in company with teaching Alexie. Spoken-word or performance poetry and slam—a competition in which judges chosen at random from the audience give poems scores while raucous audience participation is encouraged and expected (Bruce and Davis; Evans-Lynn)—offer impressive displays of skill with language and performance art. Slams also "provide lessons in perspective, in paying attention to all sides of an issue, and in realizing that there is more than one side," reports coauthor Umphrey following attendance at a slam at the Nuyorican Café in New York City.[2] We have also found that performing poetry in the classroom helps students learn that language has the "raw power and potential to quash potential acts of violence with words . . . and acts as violence intervention" (Bruce and Davis 122), an approach that points directly to themes addressed by Alexie. This chapter provides strategies for helping students use words to "make sense in a world that won't" (*Slam*) through poetry writing and slam-style spoken-word performance.

Sherman Alexie: Poet, Performer, and Performance

Alexie, the only four-time winner of the Heavyweight Poetry Bout Championships, retired from poetry competition in 2001 after winning against some remarkable poets (see http://minorheron. org/poetry-videos-heavyweight-championship.htm). All the poets Alexie bested are accomplished literary poets and slam champions, which speaks to Alexie's exceptional performance abilities. Poet Diane Thiel interviewed Alexie about his strategies for making a poem come alive. Alexie responded that storytellers were telling stories long before they had the means to record them or to write them down, so performance for him is and feels primal:

> As a storyteller, I . . . feel a responsibility to my audience. I want them to feel as strongly about the work as I do. . . . If a poem is funny, I want to hear the laughter. If it's sad, I want to hear the tears. . . . We've got a lot of competition out there in the world. I have to be at least as good as Eminem or I'm dead! . . . As a public performer, I "act." . . . I become a slightly larger and more exaggerated version of myself. (Thiel par. 24)

We have found it helpful to develop multidimensional interpretations of Alexie's poetic style through student applications of spoken-word dramatic performance and slam and to practice using poetry to speak up and out about matters of importance. These approaches not only facilitate interactive learning but also help students experience the primal nature of poetry to which Alexie refers.

We begin by directing students to the LitSite Alaska website, which posts some middle and high school native Alaskan students' reactions to an Alexie visit (http://litsite.alaska.edu/aktraditions/nativepride/alexei.html). Following one of Alexie's electrifying performances, these students seized an opportunity to have dinner with Alexie (sans adults) and later to attend a "craft talk." Alexie encouraged these students to be strong, to reach for their goals, to read, to write, to tell the truth, and to get their message out there (*LitSite Alaska* par. 3–5). We want our students to do the same.

Starting with Poetic Interpretation

Prereading: Activating Background Knowledge

The most common images of Native Americans circulating in the Montana media are those of Indians dressed in powwow regalia. Rarely do local media publish images of contemporary Indians dressed like the rest of us in jeans or business attire. Apparently, images of Indians in powwow regalia elicit nostalgia for the noble savage and represent depictions of Natives that a mostly Anglo audience finds recognizable and palatable—as a beautiful spectacle, something under control.

Alexie confronts the problematic legacy of the powwow in many of his poems in *The Business of Fancydancing*. In "Powwow Polaroid" (*Old Shirts and New Skins* 43), he addresses whether the powwow is a sellout to the commercial conception of the Indian or an opportunity to reestablish tribal ties between extended family. For Alexie, the powwow alternately is "a mode of cultural resistance or of conformity. On the negative side, the powwow makes the Indian the object of the tourist's gaze." On the positive side, "the tourist aspect of the fancydancing event is overshadowed by an affirmation of community" (Gillan 106–7). By reading "Powwow Polaroid" with our students, we all contemplate with Alexie the complications involved in negotiating competing cultural backgrounds while students begin to consider the value of poetic interpretation through dramatization as a tool for (paracolonial) resistance and (individual, social) transformation.

With students who have no familiarity at all with Native American powwows, viewing videos of fancydancing and other powwow dances helps accomplish our goals for interpreting the poem. Clips of fancydancing from Sherman Alexie's film *The Business of Fancydancing* provide relevant background reference; other films are also available that document powwow dances (check out Full Circle Videos or Oyate). We also have paired our reading of "Powwow Polaroid" with Alexie's poem "Glossary of a Powwow" from *The Summer of Black Widows* to give students a basis for understanding, interpretation, and critique.

Because the title of the poem itself is apt to reaffirm stereotypical interpretations that we have worked to deconstruct, we want to interrogate images raised in "Powwow Polaroid." We ask students to respond to the prompt "What ideas, images, questions, issues, stories, struggles, conflicts, oppositions come to mind when you read the title?" By juxtaposing their responses with the images in "Glossary of a Powwow," we are able to begin reading, albeit with the disconcerting imbalance typical of readers confronting the inadequacies of personal experience in understanding Alexie. We work several days, even weeks, on the activities described.

Reading to Understand, Reading to Interpret

Powwow Polaroid

We were fancydancing, you see.
Step-step, right foot, step-step, left foot, faster, twisting, turning, spinning, changing.

There are photographs taken but only one ever captured the
change. It was a white tourist from Spokane. She was lucky, she was
quick, maybe it was film developed by the CIA.

She took the picture, the flashbulb burned, and none of us could
move. I was frozen between steps, my right foot three inches off the
ground, my mouth open and waiting to finish the last sound.

The crowd panicked. Most fled the stands, left the dancers not
dancing and afraid. The white woman with the camera raised her
arms in triumph, crossed her legs at the ankle, tilted her head to one
side.

My four-hundred pound aunt wept into the public address system.
My uncle held his great belly in his hands, walked among the
fancydancers, said this:

forgiveness.

—Sherman Alexie, from *Old Shirts and New Skins*

The speaker in "Powwow Polaroid" describes the impact of all
the black-and-white photographs, most widely circulated in the
1906–1930 images of Edward Curtis,[3] "that fixed their Indian
subjects forever in mock-ceremonial poses. As these tourist images were commodified, Indians were expected to embody them.
The speaker in the poem describes the effect of being shot by one
tourist's camera" (Gillan 107).

We discuss Alexie's uses of historical reality—in this instance,
the exploitation that Native Americans have endured since the
invention of the camera from white photographers who have sold
Native images for exorbitant amounts of money with no compensation to the subject, as well as questionable tactics used by
the CIA to gather intelligence on members of the American
Indian Movement—and Alexie's uses of imagery and metaphor.
"Powwow Polaroid" also provides the opportunity to explain that
in many American Indian communities kinship bonds and the
use of familial terms such as *aunt, uncle, brother, son, sister,* and

daughter extend outward from immediate blood relations to networks of members in a particular clan and to others "adopted" into the community, so Alexie's frequent use of *cousin* or *cuz* demonstrates filial connection.

We ask students to begin to envision the landscape of this poem by sketching images of power, struggle, and opposition that appear in their imaginations as we read. For inspiration, we play powwow music to accompany drawing. Following the initial writing and drawing, we pair up and share writing and sketches. When conversation lulls in pairs, volunteers share writing, sketches, and/or conversation with the whole class. From this discussion, we build a chart on the board to depict what we currently know, assume, or imagine about the content of the poem and about the sociocultural and power issues Alexie is addressing.

We adapt one of Sheridan Blau's literature workshops to our first reading of the poems. We ask students to read the poems three times and

> to notice what you notice, which is to say notice what you find interesting or troubling or difficult to understand in the poem, what you like about what it says, what you might want to speak against in it, what questions you have about it or any line in it, or anything else you happen to observe or feel as a reader. (36)

At the end of each reading, as recommended by Blau, we direct students to do two additional things: (1) rate their understanding of the poem on a scale of 0 to 10 (0 = I don't get it at all; 10 = I totally get it), and (2) make some notes on what they noticed as they read. After the final reading, we ask them to repeat the routine but also to do two additional things: (1) write a brief story of their experience as a reader in terms of understanding the poem over the course of their three readings, and (2) write out any remaining questions they have about the poem (36).

Then we break from Blau's workshop and a few volunteers read the poem aloud. This gives us an idea of the varied readings or interpretations students make of the poem at this point; we also discuss how interpretation might affect performance choices readers make. To discuss Alexie's rhetoric of race identities and relations, we shift directions a bit and follow Goebel's suggestions for reading Alexie's poetry. Goebel poses a set of questions from which readers contextualize their responses to Alexie's poem. Students write briefly in reading logs in response to these questions, keeping in mind their initial impressions cataloged on the chart and questions that remain for them following their initial readings, "noticings," "wonderings," and "resistances" (either the reader's or Alexie's):

1. What are your personal responses to the . . . poem[s]? Did you like it? Why or why not? What parts appealed to you most? How does the piece make you feel? Why? What passages particularly evoke that feeling? What did you find most interesting or puzzling about the piece?

2. How does Alexie construct Native American identity within the piece? What qualities or characteristics are exhibited by the persona or characters? If applicable, how does Alexie make use of stereotype and/or the rhetoric of race in this construction of identity? . . . (Feel free to respond to other themes or topics as you see them emerge.)

3. How would you describe Alexie's style? What words or phrases does Alexie repeat? What interesting syntax or word arrangements do you notice? How does Alexie make use of figurative language? How would you describe the formal structure of the piece? How

might the style and form contribute to our understanding of the content? (144)

Students once again rate their understanding of the poem following responses to these questions. Students then gather into groups of three to four to discuss their noticings, wonderings, questions, resistances, and ratings at different points in their reading, their responses to Alexie's poem, his construction of Native American identity and white identity, and his uses of language. We steer students through a politically motivated close reading of the text by asking them to consider what they noticed about power; about oppositions; about resistance; about Alexie's particular articulations of classed, raced, and gendered interests; and about the needs, desires, and aspirations of embattled social groups represented in the actions of the personae in the poem and in the popular imagination (Dimitriadis and McCarthy 42).

Students then compare their initial impressions of the title in writing and images with their impressions of "Powwow Polaroid" at this point in our work. After that, students finish the following prompt four times using four different topic ideas that may range from literal or concrete interpretations to metaphorical or abstract interpretations:

"Powwow Polaroid" is a poem about . . .

Students take turns reading aloud their first response either in small groups or with the entire class (depending on its size), then their second, third, and fourth responses. Following this read-around, we again discuss what we notice about our interpretations of the poem, about what Alexie might be saying about power and resistance, and about any insights experienced and questions that remain.

Next, we introduce dramatic interpretation as another avenue for making sense of the poem. Students work in groups of five or six. We prompt them first to identify the characters both extant and implied in "Powwow Polaroid" (e.g., speaker, fancydancers, white tourist from Spokane/photographer, CIA agent, members of the audience, speaker's four-hundred-pound aunt, speaker's uncle) and to recount the events of the poem, thinking in terms of a beginning, middle, and end. Each group divvies up various roles constructed in the poem, gets individually into those roles, and, as a group, creates an interpretive or improvisational "instant replay" of the poem. Groups may consider sequences that portray a literal or a multilayered interpretation through which they express an emotion, a historical parallel, a metaphoric representation, actual events, or points of tension as physically described by the poem. Groups may also take up the politics of the poem and try to represent them dramatically.

Before freeing up groups to accomplish this work, we briefly consider possible dramatic strategies for bringing images to life, such as use of sound effects (hands, feet, voice), possibilities for narration, choral reading of parts of the poem or added improvised dialogue, use of tableau to freeze action while one character speaks outside the scene, tapping characters on the shoulder to bring them in and out of the scene, etc. For example, the group might freeze in tableau while "the white tourist from Spokane" recites an interior monologue spoken as lines from a letter home telling about the photographic moment at the powwow or as lines from a memo to an art dealer describing the photographic image now for sale to the highest bidder. Students see immediately the possibilities for varied interpretations and then get into roles, develop scenarios, create improvisational dialogue, determine direction and focus of dramatic scenes, and decide how to act out the poem in instant replay. After practicing together, each group takes a turn dramatizing the poem for the rest of the class.

Postreading: Synthesis, Reflection, Extension

We complete our study of "Powwow Polaroid" by writing any noticings, wonderings, or resistances in reading response journals. We discuss general impressions and understandings of the poem and how our interpretations developed through various activities and through performance. We notice attributes of strong performances and talk about ways to incorporate those strategies in our own work. We look at instances of critical thought and action that might arise from this confluence of textual production, visual art, and performance-based practices that trouble neat understanding of the text. We also discuss Alexie's construction of a resistant rhetoric of race. Students in role tend to find deeper meanings for the poem because they are able to look outside their own life contexts, move into drama, and put themselves in an imagined world.

For example, one group, in a professional development class we taught with our colleague Laurie Smith Small-Waisted Bear— herself a fifth-generation descendant of a survivor of Wounded Knee—chose to interpret "Powwow Polaroid" dramatically against the backdrop of the Wounded Knee Massacre of 1890, the tourist's flashing camera replaced by Hotchkiss artillery. As one participant improvised sounds of artillery "flashed" in a vocalized "boom, boom, boom," Rick—a six-foot-plus, barrel-chested Blackfeet guy who had brought his Chihuahua with him to class that day—lay on the floor to represent those killed at Wounded Knee while another of their colleagues recited lines from the poem. The little dog was so distressed at the dramatization that he stood on Rick's chest barking and licking his face throughout the performance. The combined gravity and hilarity of the performance emancipated the whole story of "Powwow Polaroid" through a surreal postmodern pastiche, not to be recolonized, resentimentalized, nor taken too seriously. We were certain Alexie would have approved.

Improvisation becomes a tool for exploring the poem's ideas, relationships, and language—a living-through its concepts. As David Booth explains, drama helps readers distance their own cultural frames and see new insights into the poem by putting themselves in the roles of the "characters," which brings to their interpretations new layers of meaning that deepen and enrich understanding of the poem. Students tend to lose themselves in their performance roles, which builds understanding and confidence in interpretive analysis and empathy in understanding people different from themselves.

Practicing Performance: Dramatic Literacy

We next work with students on writing and performing poems using Alexie's poems as models. Many comprehensive books written for teachers about teaching spoken-word poetry performance and slam are available and provide detailed lesson plans for accomplishing performative goals, objectives, and assessments.[4] Performance poetry in the classroom, according to Sara Holbrook and Michael Salinger is "more than just words come to life, it is life come to words"; whether the poetry, like Alexie's, be "confessional, an indictment of political and social norms, or just verbal slapstick, the audience and the writer/performer connect with a sense of real-world intimacy" (xxii).

Following Holbrook and Salinger, we scaffold paired writing and performance activities to build on one another and to help students "develop clarity in their oral communication skills" (xxvii). Their scaffolding of paired skills from which we draw follows:

Writing	Performance
■ Imagery and visual language	■ Voice projection
■ Metaphor	■ Movement
■ Memoir	■ Voice dynamics and articulation
■ Character study	■ Persona performance
■ Point of view	■ Performance for two voices
■ Collaborative writing	■ Group performance

Our protocol throughout this poetry and performance unit is first to read, then to write, and then to perform so that students are working with Alexie's material alongside their own—reading, writing, responding, and getting immediate feedback about the effectiveness of their writing through oral presentation, performance, and audience response. During the process, students workshop and revise their interpretations and writing to fit expectations of oral presentation and performance, which in turn symbiotically reshuffles as performances are revised to fit the written work (Holbrook and Salinger xxvi).

Writing from Models: Sestina and Villanelle

Although Alexie can certainly be defined as a free verse poet, he has always worked in traditional and invented forms. Alexie says his earliest interest in formalism came from individual poems rather than specific poets. Andrew Marvell's "To His Coy Mistress," Theodore Roethke's "My Papa's Waltz," Gwendolyn Brooks's "We Real Cool," and Langston Hughes's "A Dream Deferred" are formal poems Alexie admired. "Speaking both seriously and facetiously," he reports, "I think I've spent my whole career rewriting 'My Papa's Waltz' with an Indian twist" (qtd. in Thiel par. 10).

Many of Alexie's poems use traditional forms such as the sonnet, sestina, and villanelle—with end rhyme, a tenuous dance with meter, and explicit form. Alexie says,

> I've discovered that in writing toward that end rhyme, that accented or unaccented syllable, or that stanza break, I am constantly surprising myself with new ideas, new vocabulary, and new ways of looking at the world. The conscious use of form seems to have freed my subconscious. (qtd. in Thiel par. 10)

Many of Alexie's poems draw on repetition and elliptical style refrains common in both the sestina and the villanelle, which he attributes to the sanctity of repetition in his tribe and in the Native American world more generally. Repetition appeals to him both on a spiritual level and on a simple musical level. He wants his poems to sound like tribal songs (see the title poem from *One Stick Song*), which tend to go on for hours. With repetition, Alexie says, he can sometimes make English sound like Salish, the Spokane's native language. He also thinks that in terms of spirituality and prayer, "repetition can sound a note of desperation. Think of Hopkins, 'Pitched past pain.' God can feel so far away. So we sinful slobs have to keep screaming until God pays attention" (qtd. in Thiel par. 17). Alexie's poems give our students inspiration to find ways to express ideas of significance to them—"ways of crying out to 'god,'" or however our students may perceive the spiritual, unearthly, metaphysical beyond or divine.

Alexie's formal poems lend themselves as models for both writing and performance. Our students actually love working with form. Expecting resistance, we initially tried a gradual introduction to formal elements and forms such as the sonnet because rhyme and repetition lend themselves so nicely to performance. Surprisingly, we found students asking for other forms they might try. Students who consider themselves writers like the challenges a form throws their way. For students who don't, the form is a comfort. We always emphasize the idea that students have to come up with only a few really strong lines (for villanelles) and six good words (for sestinas) rather than a whole poem full of unique ideas, which tends to relieve anxiety. Students often find greater success with the villanelle at first. They find the sestina fun too, but it's a bit more challenging to sustain the form over its seven stanzas and harder to polish in final form as a performance piece.

We introduce sestinas and villanelles to our students by looking at examples of Alexie's, which highlight the ways in which his work combines the personal with the historical and political:

> Indians are politicized from birth. I was five or six years old, standing in line to get free government food on the reservation, when I had my first political thought: "Hey, I'm in this line because I'm an Indian!" . . . I was having a great time in that line with my very funny and highly verbose siblings and parents . . . [s]o I was taught to fuse the political and the artistic, the poem and the punchline. . . . In terms of love, I was involved in a long-term . . . affair with a white woman, and our races and our political positions were always a subject of discussion and dissent. I am never, not even in my most intimate moments, completely free of my tribe. (qtd. in Thiel par. 14)

We discuss these content issues as preview to Alexie's use of sestinas. We select from the myriad prereading and during-reading exercises described in this chapter to help students read to understand and to interpret through writing, discussing, and performing.

Inside Dachau

1. big lies, small lies

Having lied to our German hosts about our plans
for the day, Diane and I visited Dachau
instead of searching for rare albums in Munich.
Only a dozen visitors walked through the camp
because we were months away from tourist season.
The camp was austere. The museum was simple.

Once there, I had expected to feel simple
emotions: hate, anger, sorrow. That was my plan.
I would write poetry about how the season
of winter found a perfect home in cold Dachau.
I would be a Jewish man who died in the camp.
I would be the ideal metaphor. Munich

would be a short train ride away from hell. Munich
would take the blame. I thought it would all be simple
but there were no easy answers inside the camp.
The poems still took their forms, but my earlier plans
seemed so selfish. What could I say about Dachau
when I had never suffered through any season

inside its walls? Could I imagine a season
of ash and snow, of flames and shallow graves? Munich
is only a short train ride from Dachau.
If you can speak some German, it is a simple
journey which requires coins and no other plans
for the day. We lied about visiting the camp

to our German hosts, who always spoke of the camp
as truthfully as they spoke about the seasons.
Dachau is still Dachau. Our hosts have made no plans
to believe otherwise. As we drove through Munich
our hosts pointed out former Nazi homes, simply
and quickly. "We are truly ashamed of Dachau,"

Mikael said, "but what about all the Dachaus
in the United States? What about the death camps
in your country?" Yes, Mikael and Veronika, you ask simple
questions which are ignored, season after season.
Mikael and Veronika, I'm sorry we lied about Munich
and Dachau. I'm sorry we lied about our plans.

Inside Dachau, you might believe winter will never end. You might
   lose faith in the change of seasons
because some of the men who built the camps still live in Argentina,
   in Washington, in Munich.
They live simple lives. They share bread with sons and daughters who
   have come to understand the master plan.

—Sherman Alexie, from The Summer of Black Widows

"Inside Dachau" is a seven-part poem. Alexie has written frequently about genocidal similarities between the post-Columbus experiences of American Indians and those of European Jews during the Holocaust. His concerns, like the themes of "Inside Dachau," focus on the hypocrisy of acknowledging Nazi wrongdoing while ignoring American Indian genocide. (1) *big lies, small lies*, the introductory sestina, is followed by (2) *history as a home movie*; (3) *commonly asked questions*, a villanelle; (4) *the american indian holocaust museum*; (5) *songs from those who love the flames*; (6) *after we are free*; (7) *below freezing*, a villanelle:

7. below freezing

Dachau was so cold I could see my breath	(Aª—refrain)
so I was thankful for my overcoat.	(b)
I have nothing new to say about death.	(Aᵇ—refrain)
Each building sat at right angles to the rest.	(a)
Around each corner, I expected ghosts.	(b)
Dachau was so cold I could see my breath.	(Aª—refrain)

Everything was clean, history compressed	(a)
into shoes, photographs, private notes.	(b)
I have nothing new to say about death.	(A^b—refrain)

Everything was clean, history compressed   (a)
into shoes, photographs, private notes.   (b)
I have nothing new to say about death.   (A^b—refrain)

I wanted to weep. I wanted to rest   (a)
my weary head as the ash mixed with snow.   (b)
Dachau was so cold I could see my breath.   (A^a—refrain)

I am not a Jew. I was just a guest   (a)
in that theater which will never close.   (b)
I have nothing new to say about death.   (A^b—refrain)

I wonder which people will light fires next   (a)
and which people will soon be turned to smoke.   (b)
Dachau was so cold I could see my breath.   (A^a—refrain)
I have nothing new to say about death.   (A^b—refrain)

Following extensive discussion of our readings, understand-ings, interpretations, and performances of the poems—taking care not to rush too quickly from aesthetic and emotional responses to discussions of writer's craft—we ask students, if they haven't already noticed, if they detect anything in particular about the forms. Many pick out rhyme patterns and repetition of certain lines and Alexie's use of punctuation and enjambment—sentence syntax carried on from one line to the next, including movement from one stanza to the next—which opens conversation about the forms of sestinas and villanelles.

Sestina

A sestina is a form of sixes and "seems like the ideal writing ex-periment for a mathematical mind" (Padgett 170). Sestinas have six unrhymed stanzas of six lines each in which words at the ends of the first stanza's lines recur in a rolling pattern at the ends of all other lines. A sestina concludes with a tercet, a three-line final stanza, known as an envoi—"literally, a farewell or conclusion" (Bishop 292)—in which all six end words are used two to a line (Padgett 170).

It is easiest to see the pattern by plotting out Alexie's *big lies, small lies* on a chart (see Figure 4.1).

We examine other Alexie sestinas as models, including both the title poem and "Spokane Tribal Celebration, September 1987" from *The Business of Fancydancing*; "Dignity" from *Dangerous Astronomy*, and "Physical Education" and "The Naming of Indian Boys" from *Old Shirts and New Skins*.

We prompt students to write sestinas by encouraging them to choose their six words first. It is helpful if some are homonyms or can be used as multiple parts of speech—noun and verb, ad-

Stanza 1	Stanza 2	Stanza 3	Stanza 4	Stanza 5	Stanza 6	Envoi
1 A plans	6 F simple	3 C Munich	5 E season	4 D camp	2 B Dachaus	1,2 A,B Dachau, seasons*
2 B Dachau	1 A plan	6 F simple	3 C Munich	5 E seasons	4 D camps	3,4 C,D camps, Munich
3 C Munich	5 E season	4 D camp	2 B Dachau	1 A plans	6 F simple	5,6 E,F simple, plan*
4 D camp	2 B Dachau	1 A plans	6 F simple	3 C Munich	5 E season	*Alexie alters the typical 1,2 A,B envoi pattern to
5 E season	4 D camp	2 B Dachau	1 A plans	6 F simply	3 C Munich	convey his intended meaning. Students should
6 F simple	3 C Munich	5 E season	4 D camp	2 B Dachau	1 A plans	know poets often modify the envoi form.

Figure 4.1. Pattern chart for Alexie's sestina *big lies, small lies*.

jective or adverb. Some find it easier first to plot out the words in the end pattern and write from there. Others just write something and find their six words in that, then think of the words to go before them in the remaining stanzas. Students see that writing about something significant and evocative helps keep them from getting stuck by formal requirements and moves their writing forward.

Villanelle

The villanelle, such as *below freezing* from "Inside Dachau," contains a total of nineteen lines in six stanzas. The first five stanzas are made up of tercets (three lines). The final stanza is a quatrain (four lines). Villanelles turn on two rhymes and build around two refrains—"the first line and last line of the first stanza take turns repeating as the final line of the next four stanzas, and then are rejoined as the last two lines of the poem" (Padgett 197). An *aba* rhyme scheme is used, except in the last stanza. This is easier to understand when plotted. Examine the notations following *below freezing* above.

Students might also try plotting Alexie's villanelles "Sugar Town" from *One Stick Song* and "Poem" from *Old Shirts and New Skins*. In the villanelle "Sugar Town," Alexie autobiographically addresses the epidemic of diabetes among Indian people, a health problem the result of both genetics that prevent absorption of gluten and the preponderance of processed white flour in commodity foods. Alexie slightly alters the villanelle pattern in "Sugar Town" by using a new *b* rhyme scheme midway, yet he maintains its key components. The villanelle "Poem" draws from the historic event of forced Indian removal from Native homelands to Indian territory (now Oklahoma) known as the Trail of Tears and from contemporary problems of alcoholism, addressing both historical realities and stereotypes. Our students respond to both the solemn content and the form.

We recommend that students begin writing the villanelle by thinking of something they feel strongly about and then writing two lines that are approximately the same length and that rhyme. After students have tinkered until pleased with the result, these lines become refrains A^a and A^b. Then we encourage students to let their heads and hearts dance around with the other lines of the poem: "Writing a villanelle is like working a jigsaw puzzle; you can move the lines around until they finally seem to fit, to make a kind of poetic sense" (Padgett 199).

Students are able to write effective sestinas and villanelles modeled on Alexie's powerful content and use of formal craft by juxtaposing details and experiences from their own lives, which moves them toward powerful, passionate performances. Students discover that they can play with forms as if they were taking up a serious game or challenge—using language in certain rhythms; diving into dictionaries and thesauruses to find the perfect rhymes; crafting precise, memorable refrains; and juggling words until the form itself is rendered invisible and the dramatic outcome stands on the power and performance of the poem.

Staging Poetry Performance

By this point, students have worked hard to write, revise, and perform their poems in class. We have looked at some of Alexie's performances available on video (http://www.minorheron.org/poetry-videos-heavyweight-championship.htm) and on the Web (e.g., http://poetryfoundation.org/publishing/aroundtheweb.html) to further analyze and apply performance techniques. Students are now ready to plan and stage a poetry performance or series of events outside the classroom to continue to improve their writing and performance communication skills in a real-world context; they are ready for a public audience to push them to produce their best work and give them a tangible event toward which to polish their performance skills. *Outspoken!* (Holbrook and Salinger) and *The Complete Idiot's Guide to Slam Poetry* (Smith and Kraynak) offer comprehensive advice for staging public poetry events and competitions, as does the article "Slammin'" by Lorilee Evans-Lynn.

We have found that the context of Alexie's poetry opens doors for our students to explore with heartfelt passion the day-to-day realities of their complex concerns about humanity in all its injustice and vainglory. Spoken-word performance poetry and slam provide opportunities for young poets' voices to evoke the clear high note of anguish at the injustice of racism experienced in the here and now, the pain of suffering as a target of homophobia, or the joys of falling in love and sorrow at its loss. Tackling such issues helps our students to convey profound insight, inspires provocative performance, and motivates empathy. As students learn poetic diction, forms, and other devices for creating powerful imagery, emotive language, and riveting performance techniques, they realize that finding strong words and oratorical devices to express more artfully their anger or dismay or joy is much more interesting and engaging than more typical means deployed in contemporary popular culture. Alexie's poetry and performance panache provide exemplary models.

Notes

1. Heavyweight Poetry Bout Championships were sponsored by the World Poetry Bout Association from 1982 to 2003 in Taos, New Mexico, at the Taos Poetry Circus, which folded its tent in 2003.

2. The distinction between a poetry bout and a slam is slight but significant. In a poetry bout, two poets face off against each other reading a previously published or extemporaneous poem in round, like a boxing

match. Poets read previously written poems for the first nine rounds; in the last round, each poet draws a word and extemporaneously makes up a poem about that word. Poets in a bout are scored by three judges, who pick a winner. Slams similarly blend poetry, performance, and competition in theatrical, street-easy style; however, unlike poetry bouts, which were star-studded invitational events that featured well-known poets, slams are open to all—young and old, published and unpublished—and more suited to our purposes with students.

3. Between 1906 and 1930, Edward Curtis published a twenty-volume photographic collection, *The North American Indian*, "to document tribal culture in the United States before it vanished" (Gillan 110).

4. Our favorites because of their resourceful practicality are *Outspoken! How to Improve Writing and Speaking Skills through Poetry Performance* (Holbrook and Salinger) and *Brave New Voices: The YOUTH SPEAKS Guide to Teaching Spoken Word Poetry* (Weiss and Herndon). We also like John O'Connor's *Wordplaygrounds: Reading, Writing, and Performing Poetry in the English Classroom* and, for teachers of younger students, Nancie Atwell's *Naming the World: A Year of Poems and Lessons*.

5 Reservation (Sings the) *Blues*

Sherman Alexie's first novel, *Reservation Blues*, is well worth teaching to high school students. It offers students an appealing introduction to Native American literatures through its contemporary topics and humor. It is also compelling because of its enigmatic references to history, pop culture, and music as well as its literally larger-than-life characters such as Big Mom and the-man-who-is-probably-Lakota. The novel's broad readability is another asset to consider. For teachers looking to lead discussions of theme, literary devices, and racial stereotyping, *Reservation Blues* has plenty to offer.

We have, however, encountered students who profess to love *Smoke Signals*, Alexie's first feature-length film, as well as his poetry, but who confess not to understand his prose. As accessible as his writing is on a basic sentence level, the organization of his ideas can be daunting. Like other Native American writers, Alexie treats time as event-focused and contained rather than as chronologically linear, a sense of time with which many of our non-Native students are unfamiliar, hence their difficulties. Alexie tends, for example, to surge ahead to new events and characters suddenly and then wash back over how one scene fits with the rest, how characters arrived there, how the plot has unfolded to that point. Non-Native readers might compare Alexie's prose to that of William Faulkner's "A Rose for Emily." Long a staple of high school literature, this short story makes similar chronological twists. This quality, combined with potentially unfamiliar historical, pop culture, and music references, as well as literary devices such as hyperbole and surrealism, can make *Reservation Blues* confusing or even incomprehensible to some of our students. Most of them need background information before they begin as well as guidance as they read this book.

What makes *Reservation Blues* a joy to teach on a reservation is its constant connection to aspects of reservation life, both positive and negative: tradition, commodities, HUD houses, frybread. Yet readers unfamiliar with these universal characteristics of Indian country may not appreciate Alexie's humor or his revealing commentary about the culture. Therefore, teachers of students located far from reservations will likely need to provide a glossary or explanations of unknown words and concepts,[1] just as modern educators must do when teaching Shakespeare or as we have to do when teaching "A Rose for Emily," set in the Deep South around the turn of the century. Coauthor Anna Baldwin had the following conversation with one of her students after the class read *Reservation Blues*:

MRS. BALDWIN: "Do you think people who don't live on a reservation would have trouble understanding this book?"

JOE: "Very much. . . . They wouldn't understand why [the characters] live in a HUD house or drink commodity grape juice, or how they talk."

Another potential obstacle is shallow character development. We address this shortcoming by spending a lot of time discussing characters' motives, their pasts, and their choices. The character diary, described below, helps students imagine the mind of at least one character. We might even have a conversation about why Alexie developed his characters so thinly and brainstorm ideas about how he could have intensified them.

Every novel presents teachers with challenges, whether those be an author's use of elevated language, a setting in unfamiliar country, or use of unorthodox structure or modern themes untested by a seasoned teacher. The strengths of *Reservation Blues* lie in how it pushes both teachers and students alike. When readers decode reservation culture as depicted by Alexie, unlock the mysteries of the novel's literary devices, and unravel the tangled timelines, they will have wrestled out the best of this book and come through as better students and more effective teachers.

Returning to the Roots of American Music: The Blues and Robert Johnson

We begin teaching this novel by introducing students to the nature of the blues through an easy-to-read, brief description of blues music and culture, including its geographic roots and its main figures, legends such as Muddy Waters and B. B. King. An excellent source is the PBS blues website, which describes Martin Scorsese's documentary about the blues. In particular, the essay "What Is the Blues?" by W. C. Handy provides an interesting and succinct introduction (http://www.pbs.org/theblues/classroom/essaysblues.html). As a class, we discuss themes found in the blues—the difficulties of life, loneliness, and desertion by loved ones. Most students know a little about the blues, but many do not care for the musical style. Our goal is to provide enough information that students can answer the prereading question, "What do you think a novel titled *Reservation Blues* might be about?"

Because the first character we meet in the novel is Robert Johnson, students must understand the importance of this mysterious figure in American music history. We have sometimes shown the documentary *The Search for Robert Johnson* (1992), directed by Chris Hunt, which traces Johnson's life, family, and the strange circumstances of his death at a young age. This film also describes the life of bluesmen, depicting the landscape and people of the Mississippi Delta country, the birthplace of the blues.

We provide copies of the lyrics of "Crossroad Blues" and discuss the story of the crossroads, a legend that has arisen in many cultures since the time of Robert Johnson. In this legend, a musician sells his soul to the devil in exchange for talent and success. One verse laments,

> Standin' at the crossroads, risin' sun goin' down
> Standin' at the crossroads baby, the risin' sun goin' down
> I believe to my soul now, po' Bob is sinkin' down.

Students have no trouble identifying Eric Clapton, who remade the song; the appearance of the legend in the film *O Brother, Where Art Thou*; and a rap song called "Tha Crossroads" by Bone Thugs-N-Harmony. When asked how a person can earn his soul back, at least one student will offer as evidence the song "The Devil Went Down to Georgia" by the Charlie Daniels Band. Over time, we have collected the lyrics and audio versions of all these songs to play in order to bring the lesson to life.

All this background development takes about two class periods and helps animate the first few lines of *Reservation Blues*, which describe Robert Johnson standing at the crossroads on the Spokane Indian Reservation.

Early Reading: Theme Discussion

Several recurring themes arise in *Reservation Blues*, which can make for interesting book talks and essays. We provide questions for thinking and discussion during or after chapter discussions to prompt students to think about the importance of music, the effects of poverty, the symbolism of water, and the influence of alcoholism, all primary themes in the novel. Some sample questions include:

- The-man-who-is-probably-Lakota says, "Music is a dangerous thing" (12). How might music be dangerous? Who might think so? Who might disagree?
- About Junior, "None of his siblings had enough money to mourn properly" (24). Why would someone need money in order to mourn? Describe how poverty affects these people's lives in a fundamental way.
- Water is often considered a purifier. What significances might we attribute to Junior's job driving a water truck and delivering water to the West End, which "ran out of water every summer" (16)?
- "Junior never drank until the night of his high school graduation. He'd sworn never to drink because of his parents' boozing. Victor placed a beer gently in his hand, and Junior drained it without hesitation or question" (57). Why did Junior wait until that night to drink a beer? Why do you think he no longer hesitated?

Early Reading: Surrealism and Hyperbole

Part of the confusion many students experience with Alexie's prose is his free use of hyperbole and surrealism, usually with no warning or explanation. Students unfamiliar with surrealism may have trouble deciphering a description such as "Music rose above the reservation, made its way into the clouds, and rained down" (24).

And what are they to make of the next description if they have never heard of hyperbole? "Victor grew extra fingers that roared up and down the fingerboard. He bent strings at impossible angles and hit a note so pure that the guitar sparked. The sparks jumped from the guitar to a sapling and started a fire" (78). Our remedy is to teach the definitions of each term and give examples from other sources as we cover the first chapter. Other literary examples are fine, as are those we might invent on the spot. We make certain to distinguish between clichés such as "I'm so hungry I could eat a horse" and Alexie's more refined, nuanced expressions.

Paintings help explain surrealism; the work of Salvador Dalí in particular comes to mind. As we discuss the novel in class, we are careful to point out examples of each device early on and then ask students to find examples from a chapter to share. We ask them to rewrite the hyperbolic language in less exaggerated prose so they can assess the effects of Alexie's words. Addie, for example, rewrote the original line "The crowds kept growing and converted the rehearsal into a semi-religious ceremony . . ." (33) to this simplified version: "The crowd got really big and excited." Reading the rewritten sentence first, followed by the original hyperbole, helps students hear how Alexie's exaggeration adds interest as well as nuanced meaning. Reading Alexie and our revisions out loud demonstrates clarity and helps students to better understand the device. We have given them opportunities to write their own examples of hyperbole or surrealism. After they become aware of these literary devices, they can spot them and avoid confusion when reading.

Mid-novel Reading: Character Diaries

As mentioned, one of the novel's weaknesses is its lack of character development. There is little revelation of any character's inner thoughts or suggestions of motives for actions, except in family histories woven throughout the novel. We offset this weakness with a character diary. After the characters Chess and Checkers are introduced (Chapter 3), students choose to focus on one of five main characters: Thomas, Victor, Junior, Chess, or Checkers; then they create a diary from the perspective of that character. Students use a sheet of construction paper for the cover and about five sheets of unlined white paper for the inside. They fold it, staple the edge, and decorate the outside the way they think their character might. The character's name goes on the front and the student's name on the back. After each reading selection (sometimes about half a chapter, sometimes a whole chapter), students write in their diaries from their chosen character's point of view. We encourage them to construct inner thoughts and feelings, interior monologues rather than plot summaries (e.g., not "Today I ate frybread for breakfast. . . ."). The diary allows students to become that character by writing what they imagine the character might be thinking but not saying, thereby deepening character development and student comprehension of the novel.

A common question that arises is "But my character doesn't have a part in this section. What should I do?" In every case, a student can make a guess about the character's feelings and thoughts about what is happening, whether that character is present in a given scene or not. These diaries require students to examine their character's personality traits and motivations and to reveal hidden ideas about these characters. They pick up where Alexie leaves off.

Mid-novel Reading: Historical References

One of the novel's enigmas is its use of real history in fictional ways. Big Mom (fictional), for example, is purported to be the music instructor of several significant rock musicians such as Janis Joplin and Jimi Hendrix. Robert Johnson is a historical figure Alexie uses in iconic and fictional ways. More interesting, however, is Alexie's use of the names Phil Sheridan and George Wright for the executives from Cavalry Records. It is important to point out that Sheridan and Wright were two American generals who conducted hostile actions against Indians during the 1860s to 1880s on behalf of the U.S. military. These historical connections will escape many students, so we provide enough background information to help students understand how these characters have secondary connections to the plot. At the least, such background will provide depth and motive to these two characters in particular and to others that Alexie uses in the novel.

Mid-novel Reading: Difficult Issues

Victor and the Priest

Many students balk at the memories Victor has of his childhood in the Catholic orphanage. Indeed, it is initially unclear whether the memories, seen in a dream, are real or imagined. Some students want to overlook or change the content of the dream. Others dismiss it: "Priests are sick!" is a comment we have heard often. This is a tough topic to tackle because of its connections to religion, current news, and stereotypes. We choose to use the theme of stereotypes as a way to address the subject because most students can talk productively about stereotyping. We discuss stereotyping as a habit, as well as stereotypes of clergy and truths about them; we talk about events covered by the news in addition to those *not* covered (typically, the positive kind). We eventually work our way into a discussion of the use of stereotypes in this novel, prompting with questions such as "Is Alexie using stereotypes to make us think one thing or another? Is he intentionally misleading us? (Why?) Is he simplifying the characters in order to make us fill in the blanks?" Usually this prediscussion enables a conversation about molestation and Victor's memories, and it paves the way for later talks about racial stereotyping.

Junior's Suicide

Chapter 9, "Small World," presents the climax of the story in reverse chronological order. It can be shocking and confusing to encounter Junior's suicide and *then* read the events preceding it. Although no real explanation is offered, students have plenty of ideas about why Junior might have ended his life. We address this chapter in two ways: first, we detangle its plot; second, we discuss and write about the suicide.

The plot is written in reverse. Segments are divided by manuscript indicators—the use of three crosses. Readers need only move backward from the end of Chapter 9 to the beginning, segment by segment, to figure out what happened in chronological order. The amount of time elapsed between events is indicated, so we ask students to form small groups to create a timeline of events. Then we put the timeline on the board so everyone can see it. It should read as follows:

1	2	3	4	5	6	7	8
Coyote Springs returns from NY.	Betty & Veronica get record deal.	Father Arnold decides to leave.	Robert J. & Big Mom talk.	Chess & Thomas decide to leave.	Victor dreams about the guitar.	Checkers goes to church.	Junior commits suicide.

The typical high school curriculum is full of stories about death: *Of Mice and Men*, *Lord of the Flies*, and *The Crucible* offer just a few examples. Not as many deal with suicide; *Romeo and*

Juliet is the most notable title. However, many of our students have faced the tragedy of the effects of suicide, often with the death of a friend or peer. We address this issue, which is an epidemic in Indian country, by moving from creation of the plot timeline to questions intended to examine both Junior's suicide and Alexie's possible intent: "Why did Alexie *start* this chapter with the death?"

Most students say he wants to shock us. Others simply add this unusual tactic to the other odd time phenomena in this chapter—the flashbacks, the chapters organized by moving both backward and forward in time. Then we ask students to respond to the obvious question, "Why did Junior do it?" And we talk about their ideas. Many students will point out that he was the smartest of the group of characters, that Junior had the most lost potential and therefore was the most likely to commit suicide. We also help students to see that Alexie might have chosen Junior's death as a way to shock his readers into thinking about the damaging effects of poverty and ongoing colonialism on rates of youth suicide in Native American communities. Many students will say they never saw it coming, while others anticipated a death but thought it would be a different character. This chapter provides teachers with opportunities to help students think about the pain and sense of loss caused by suicide.

Post-novel Essay: Themes

All through the novel, students note various themes. Several from our early reading discussion can be carried through to the end: the significance of music, dreams, poverty, and loneliness, for example. At various points throughout our reading schedule, we ask students in small groups to do a theme hunt over a chunk of about three chapters. Each group must find places in those chapters where a given theme surfaces in a meaningful way and note in their reading response journals its appearance; they identify relevant textual passages, including quotes or paraphrases, in which the theme appears, as well as the page number. As a class, we chart thematic development, and later the chart can be photocopied and used by all students as a way to find textual evidence for essays written about the novel. These essays either focus on thematic arguments or take the form of character sketches, which describe a character's motives and accomplishments; students use the character diaries to compile supporting evidence for their argument.

The Movie: What Movie?

Students who have seen *Smoke Signals* will associate it with this novel. While some events and characters are similar, the movie is not a remake of the book. We choose not to confuse students or compromise the book by showing *Smoke Signals* as a companion to reading *Reservation Blues*. Instead, if we view a film in conjunction with reading this novel, we show *Crossroads* (1986). The film and book can be compared in many ways, including the themes of music, poverty, racism, "the journey," and loneliness vs. companionship; the film hearkens back to our early discussions of the blues and includes as a significant presence the legendary Robert Johnson. The film is rated R for mild profanity. Many of today's PG-13 ratings by far surpass *Crossroads* in their violence, language, and sexual content.

Dissension

Most students who read *Reservation Blues* in class enjoy it. More than one student has confessed, "That's the only school book I ever read all the way through." Yet a few dislike it. Jason recorded his feelings in the following statement, at our request:

> Sherman Alexie often uses recurring characters in most of his work, namely Thomas and Victor. These characters usually lack depth and development, and are often stereotypical in ways that aren't positive. . . . Although I feel that the book *Reservation Blues* lacks what is needed for a good book—plot, character development, and pacing, it could be used effectively in teaching stereotypes, hyperbole, and surrealism.

Jason's mention of stereotypes identifies a source of frustration for many students. They find the depiction of alcoholism, poverty, and other societal ills in the context of reservation life disturbing. They think Alexie is reinforcing negative stereotypes. They worry that people off the reservation might read these depictions and find their beliefs about Native Americans justified; after all, this is a Native American author. We have addressed this concern in earlier chapters and in Chapter 6.

Teacher Caution

A final note about the terminology in this novel: Alexie refers to Chess and Checkers Warm Water as "Flathead" Indians. This incorrect name for the Salish people was given following the arrival of white men in the area. It is an understandable mistake since one of the reservations on which the novel takes place is called the Flathead Indian Reservation, but the Salish people do not call themselves Flatheads and ask others to respect the correct tribal name as well.[2]

Notes

1. *The Cambridge Companion to Native American Literature* edited by Joy Porter and Kenneth M. Roemer provides all the information a teacher needs to help students build necessary background information.

2. We thank Frances Vanderburg, Salish elder, for this information.

6 Taking a Critical Stance

In the inaugural volumes of the NCTE High School Literature Series, Carol Jago excerpts professional literary criticism to provide students with models of analytical writing that illustrate taking a critical stance. Her intent is to help high school writers see examples of writing they are expected to create and to provide them with interpretations that might help them refine and reconsider their own responses to literature under study. We approach our study of Sherman Alexie for reasons cited by Jago but also because we think professional criticism helps us as teachers to understand more deeply the literature we select to teach. We also like discussing critical controversies (Graff; Graff and Phelan; Richter) with our students to demonstrate that professional critics do not all reach comparable interpretations. In fact, some outright disagree, as is the case with the following excerpts about the literature and humor of Sherman Alexie.

Studying and teaching Native American literatures poses particular questions that professional criticism helps us to address. McLaughlin summarizes the primary concerns: (1) verifying authenticity of Native American authorship is essential when teaching Native American literature; and (2) most of us know very little about Native American literature due to lack of exposure; teaching Native American works without understanding their cultural and historical contexts constitutes "interpretive violence." It is essential to do our homework before we teach Native American literatures.

These claims are fraught with difficult questions that abound in Native American studies, which among others include "What makes an Indian an Indian?" "Who has the right to tell the stories?" "How do I deal with tribal specificities?" "How much historical context is necessary to understand Native American literatures?" "If I do not understand Native American literatures well enough to teach them, should I not attempt it? If I do not try, will I help perpetuate ignorance of America's first peoples?" In teaching Sherman Alexie, we also contemplate the following commonly asked questions: (1) Does Sherman Alexie have a moral vision? (2) How do you contend with Alexie's persistent use of negative stereotypes of Indian people? (3) How do you comprehend Alexie's uses of biting humor, satire, and irony? Professional criticism helps us address these important questions.

The following excerpts represent a range of commentaries and interpretations on Alexie and highlight critical response to some of the works we discuss in this volume. We also include selections that help us tackle those frequently asked questions about moral consequences, negative stereotypes, and humor. We imagine both teachers and students as possible audiences for these selections, knowing that the diction of some might give students a bit of a struggle. Such struggle helps our students engage in meaningful discussions of Alexie's work.

Readings

David L. Moore

Sherman Alexie: Irony, Intimacy, and Agency

Sherman Alexie's . . . popular persona as a comedian, poetry bout heavyweight, experimental writer, filmmaker, and social pundit has itself become a work of art. He shares with many American Indian writers a central motif reaffirming Native lives and Native nationhood, although his direct comedic style and ironic attitude set him apart from the earnest lyricism of the now canonized elder Native writers [e.g., Momaday, Silko, Erdrich]. . . . Unlike many, Alexie rarely points toward the redemptive power of Native community as a direction for his protagonists' struggles. Instead, his bold, sometimes campy, style tends to affirm a more individual agency unique to Native identities, by a distinct artistic pattern of personal affirmation and reconnection. One reviewer marks an ironic balance, writing that Alexie's "dry sincerity leavens the sentiment" of his Indian tales. For all his humor, indeed in the heart of his humor, Alexie invariably circulates the grave themes of ongoing colonial history and its personal effects in Indian country. . . . [B]ecause of the weariness of difference, Alexie's voice comes from a radical affirmation of diversity. . . .

Echoing the claims and musings of some of his fictional characters, Alexie affirmed in a conversation with President Clinton during the 1998 "Dialogue on race," televised on PBS,

> I think the primary thing that people need to know about Indians is that our identity is much less cultural now and

much more political. That we really do exist as political entities and sovereign political nations. That's the most important thing for people to understand, that we are separate politically and economically. And should be.

Alexie's emphasis on the political and legal status of tribal sovereignty, rather than the cultural dynamics of tribal life, reflects his own mixed engagement with mainstream and Native cultures. Alexie's is a populist voice, uniquely situated behind enemy lines, of both those tribal changes and that tribal sovereignty. That duality is another source of his irony . . . His comedy sparks the surprise of reconnections, and his irony refocuses connections by their lack. The affirmation is tough, facing harsh realities, but it is ultimately enlivening. As he maps the intimate psychological and social violence of Indian-white relations, he not only humanizes that history of grief, but he minimizes it by showing how humor can survive even death. . . . As Alexie explains in an interview, "These aren't happy stories necessarily. But I think they are positive stories."

David L. Moore, 2005. "Sherman Alexie: Irony, Intimacy, and Agency." *Cambridge Companion to Native American Literature*. Ed. Joy Porter and Kenneth M. Roemer. Cambridge, UK: Cambridge UP. 300–302.

▪ ▪ ▪ ▪ ▪ ▪ ▪ ▪ ▪ ▪ ▪ ▪ ▪ ▪ ▪ ▪

Elizabeth Cook-Lynn (Crow/Creek/Sioux)

The question "Who gets to tell the stories?" is a very old one, but the *New York Times* started rephrasing this question last year in regard to Native American literatures, at

least, when it discovered . . . the newly available works of
native poets, *Fire Water World* by Adrian Louis (Paiute) and
The Business of Fancydancing by Sherman Alexie (Spokane/
Coeur d'Alene), and pronounced them the new, angry warriors. . . . It's just that the unhappy, deficit model of our
lives, whether Indian or white or male or female, seems to
be unrestrained, assimilative, excessive and all-inclusive in
these works [Louis's and Alexie's] and that they are, therefore, probably best described as just the **new angry**.

I guess I should like to, then, offer a concluding answer
right now[;] . . . the concluding answer is: "Those who get
to tell the stories are the people that America wants to listen
to," a very simple declarative sentence emerging from the
sure knowledge that we live, after all, in a democracy where
the right to speak your piece is revered. America likes to
listen to the new angry warriors. Look at the Schwarzkopf
phenomenon—a best selling book, speaking engagements
across the country. I can think of several examples, but there
is probably no better nor more engaging example than the
currently popular big-mouth Rush Limbaugh[,] . . . angry,
conservative and racist, who has, I'm told, twenty-eight
million listeners every week, listeners who seem happy to
be drawn into his public confessional of hatred and anger
like its some kind of indescribable and irresistible narcotic
of our times. Perhaps it is.

Elizabeth Cook-Lynn, 1993. "Who Gets to Tell the Stories?" *Wicazo
Sa Review* 9.1: 60–61.

Sherman Alexie (Spokane/Coeur d'Alene)
In Response to Elizabeth Cook-Lynn's Pronouncement That I One of
the New, Angry (Warriors) Kind of Like Norman Schwarzkopf and
Rush Limbaugh

Walking in downtown Spokane alone, after
dinner with the Indian woman I love,
with the same Indian woman who loves me,
I was stopped by an Indian man, a stranger,

drunk, sitting in the shade, as transient
as every other Indian in the country.
"Hey, cousin," he asked. "What tribe you are?"
"Spokane/Coeur d'Alene," I said and he shook

my hand. "What's your name?" he asked and I told him.
"Hey," he said. "You're that writer.
I like some of your poems." He touched my hand
again and I touched his, not pretending to know

his exact story, but understanding how close
my life has often used the same words as his.
How easy it would have been to call him by less
than his real name, how easy it would have been

to see him as a white man in Indian skin, how
easy it would have been to make war on him.
But I tell you his name was Mark, his tribe
was Yakama, and he used to traditional dance.

You see, I want to search for grace, peace, beauty
and find it sometimes in the most ordinary
but that Yakama Indian man didn't want anything
except a quarter and I gave him a dollar.

Next time he asks you for something
how much are you going to give him?

Sherman Alexie, 1993. "In Response to Elizabeth Cook-Lynn's Pronouncement That I One of the New, Angry (Warriors) Kind of Like Norman Schwarzkopf and Rush Limbaugh." *Wicazo Sa Review* 9.2: 9.

Gloria Bird (Spokane)

. . . This review questions the assumption that because someone is Indian what they produce is automatically an accurate representation. It addresses specific problems with the construed, generic "Indian" qualities that are attributed to diverse tribal peoples. It attempts to discuss the elements of . . . *Reservation Blues* that, in the spirit of an Indian Spike Lee, contribute to a portrait of an exaggerated version of reservation life, one that perpetuates many of the stereotypes of native people and presents problems for native and non-native readers alike. . . . Alexie's *Reservation Blues* . . . attempts to invest his novel with *Indianness,* but ultimately "preys" upon a variety of native cultures along the way. The examples are numerous, and include for instance, the use of the greeting, "ya-hey," which is a contrived expression. One can only speculate that it is based upon the Diné greeting, *ya'át' ééh* (ya-tey). Mainstream readers who do not have access to native language usage, either Salish or Diné, will not have a way to make an accurate assessment of its appearance in the novel and will rely solely upon what they *read* as being representationally accurate. When we examine how stereotypes of Indian are returned to the source of their original production and the dynamics that come into play in *Reservation Blues,* the impress of colonial influence become more apparent. . . . Stereotyping native peoples does not supply a native readership with soluble ways of under-mining stereotypes, but becomes a part of the problem, and returns an image of a "generic" Indian back to the original producers of that image.

The danger is with the gross representation becoming implicit. That is, when people (who haven't grown up on an Indian reservation) decide this representation is accurate and . . . reinforce the assumption back to a general readership, who, in turn, have no empirical knowledge as a basis for comparison. . . . Exaggeration seems to be the rule (a symp-tom of postmodern literature); it is the exaggeration of de-spair without context that doesn't offer enough substance to be more than a "spoof" of contemporary reservation life. . . . The representations of Indian [that Alexie] presents to a non-native audience are also "safer," because they are dressed in America's favorite subjects when it comes to Indians: trag-edy and despair.

In denying Indians a full-fledged humanity and in pre-senting only superficial markers for the representations of Indian, [Alexie] ends up with the only other acceptable pos-sibility (for mainstream readers): the drunken Indian. . . . [T]he representation of alcoholism in *Reservation Blues*, how-ever accurate, still capitalizes upon the stereotypical image of the "drunken Indian." . . . Despite the verisimilitude of Alexie's portrayal of alcoholism and its impact upon indi-vidual lives, he does not attempt to put the social problems of economic instability, poverty, or cultural oppression into perspective. Instead, alcoholism and drinking are sensation-alized. . . . What is missing from . . . *Reservation Blues* is a sense of responsibility to the cultures [he] is attempting to represent.

Gloria Bird, 1995. "The Exaggeration of Despair in Sherman Alexie's *Reservation Blues.*" *Wicazo Sa Review* 11.2: 47-52.

■ ■ ■ ■ ■ ■ ■ ■ ■ ■ ■ ■ ■ ■ ■ ■

Stephan F. Evans

Following publication of *The Lone Ranger and Tonto* and *Reservation Blues,* . . . Alexie . . . came under fire from certain quarters for his purportedly negative use of irony and satire—namely, literary connections to (white) popular culture and representations of Indian stereotypes that some consider "inappropriate" and dangerously misleading for mainstream consumption. . . . [F]or example, Louis Owens finds that Alexie's fiction

> Too often simply reinforces all of the stereotypes desired by white readers: bleakly absurd and aimless Indians are imploding in a passion of self-destructiveness and self-loathing; there is no family or community center toward which his characters . . . might turn for coherence; and in the process of self-destruction the Indians provide Euroamerican readers with pleasurable moments of dark humor or the titillation of bloodthirsty savagery. Above all, the non-Indian reader of Alexie's work is allowed to come away with a sense . . . that no one is really to blame but the Indians, no matter how loudly the author shouts his anger. (79–80)

. . . Point well taken. But criticism along [these] lines . . . clearly denigrate and misjudge Alexie's purpose in crafting a different and fresh imaginative literary realism. . . .

Considered from another critical angle, Alexie's artistry . . . may be seen as that of a consciously moral satirist rather than as a "cultural traitor." In fact, a close examination of Alexie's work . . . shows that he uses the ameliorative social and moral values inherent in irony and satire, as well as certain conventional character types (including the prejudicial stereotype of the "drunken Indian") as materials for constructing a realistic literary document for contemporary Indian survival. . . . [T]he best moments in Alexie's poems, stories, and novels lie in his construction of a satiric mirror that reflects the painful reality of lives that have become distorted, disrupted, destroyed, and doomed by their counter-impulses to embrace or deny traditional Indian culture, to become assimilated to or resist absorption into white civilization—or both.

Neither Bird nor Cook-Lynn . . . apparently sees or is willing to credit Alexie's essentially moral aims in writing poetry and fiction that is heavily infused with irony and satire, including his ethical reversal or extension of stereotypes in order to establish new valences of imaginative literary realism. C. Hugh Holman and William Harmon's well-known and broadly inclusive definition of "satire" clearly matches the tenor of Alexie's artistic intent in fashioning realistic Indian survival literature: "A literary manner that blends a critical attitude with humor and wit for the purpose of improving human institutions or humanity. True satirists are conscious of the frailty of human institutions and attempt through laughter not so much to tear them down as to inspire a remodeling" (447). Again, much of Alexie's work . . . comprises a modern survival document from which his readers gain strength by actively participating in the recognition of reality as viewed through Alexie's satiric lens or from the reflections of his satiric mirror.

. . . [Bird] fails to credit the artistic and moral strengths that are found in Alexie's depictions of the drunken Indian.

. . . In the collaborative making of meaning between Alexie and his readers, images of the drunken Indian function as "open containers" (pun intended) to house or decant realistic valences of meaning for modern reservation life and people. These forms function positively in terms of the original notion of the term *stereotype*, or "mold"—but with an important difference. Whereas usual notions of stereotype generally reflect "commonly held and oversimplified mental pictures or judgments of a person, a race, an issue, a kind of art" (Holman and Harmon 481), Alexie's purportedly stereotypical drunken Indians achieve and convey for readers vital resonances of realism when he uses them to express the recursive, historical patterns of defeat and exploitation of Indian peoples by white civilization. . . . Alexie's moral role as a poet and fiction writer enables him to construct through imaginative literary realism a viable means for his peoples' survival—through works that are ironic, self-reflexively satiric and, at times, suffused with wit and humor. . . . [Alexie] insists on confronting, through satire and irony, the culturally embedded patterns of modern Indian defeat, of which alcohol-related problems are symptomatic. . . . There can be no mistaking that Alexie deplores self-destruction and the debasement of cultural values through alcohol. . . . [A]lcohol defeats, destroys, and is used as a coping or avoidance mechanism for confronting the harshness of reservation reality; in no way is Alexie's use of the "drunken Indian" . . . stereotypical or gratuitous.

. . . Alexie's use of stereotypes[,] . . . including prejudicial images held by whites, must be seen to take on, as his work usually does, a moral function through satire and irony: they are the "open containers" holding negative "familiar" notions of Indians that add texture and valences of meaning to [his work's] mythic dimension through their inversion, demolition, and defamiliarization. In other words, Alexie tends to turn inside out stereotypes such as the drunken Indian; refashioned through satire and irony, these "open containers" can resonate with fresh values. . . . What is of paramount importance in evaluating Alexie's satiric artistry is the fact that he uses stereotypes, like that of the drunken Indian, in new and entirely moral and ethical ways, drawing his readers in to participate with him in the creation of meaning. . . . In this way Alexie's "open containers" function as key elements in his ongoing construction, through his use of imaginative literary realism, or a viable survival document that enables his readers to cope with the issues of contemporary reservation reality.

Stephen F. Evans, 2001. "'Open Containers': Sherman Alexie's Drunken Indians." *American Indian Quarterly* 25.1: 46-72.

Ron McFarland

. . . There is a combativeness that distinguishes Alexie's often polemical poems, for he is, in a way, at war. In most of his writing, sooner or later, Alexie is a "polemicist," which is to say, "a warrior," and there is nearly always controversy and argument, implied or direct, in his poems and stories. (Clearly, I am not employing the term "polemic" pejoratively here, but I do consider that designation to be provocative.) "Do you ever worry about anger becoming a negative force?" the Bellante brothers asked [Alexie in their Bloomsbury interview]. Citing Gandhi, Alexie answered that anger could be a positive force: "Anger without hope, anger without love, or anger without compassion are all-consuming. That's not my kind of anger. Mine is very specific and directed." This is not to say that this makes his anger exactly "palatable." . . . Alexie's powers as a poet are primarily narrative, and after that rhetorical, and with that, perhaps as a sub-species, polemical.

From the foregoing it should be obvious enough that Alexie's is a rhetoric, whether in his poems or in his fiction, that reflects pain and anger, a rhetoric that could give way to bitterness. What keeps that from happening and makes the pain and anger bearable for the reader . . . is not so much the hope, love, and compassion to which he refers in the interview, but humor. Predictably, this humor is rarely gentle or playful (though it can be that at times), but most often satirical. People, white and Indian as well, laugh out loud and often when Alexie reads, and in the former case, they are frequently laughing at themselves. . . . Alexie's poems are filled with such moments of painful or poignant humor which may be described as "serious" or "dark." . . . The impact is not so much like the escape or release offered by comedy as the catharsis provided by tragedy.

Ron McFarland, 1997. "Another Kind of Violence: Sherman Alexie's Poems." *American Indian Quarterly* 21.2: 253, 263.

Taking a Stance with Alexie

Bruce Goebel's "*The Business of Fancydancing* and Postmodern Native America" (142–62), from his book *Reading Native American Literature: A Teacher's Guide*, offers close readings of selected poems and stories from *The Business of Fancydancing.* Goebel describes a critical reader and writer's journal that he uses to push students to reflect as critics on "*what* the text means, considering their personal responses, . . . the thematic concerns of the work, Alexie's construction of Native American identity, and his use of humor and the rhetoric of race" (143). His overarching prompt asks students "to offer (1) a personal response to each piece, (2) observations about such themes and topics as identity, ethnicity, family, gender, and sports, and (3) descriptions of style and form" (144). We use Goebel's critical reader and writer's journal as a jumping-off place to help our students respond as they read and as an entryway into helping them formulate a critical stance on the work of Alexie.

We don't share professional criticism with students too soon, because we want them first to formulate their own opinions without too much outside interference; we scaffold these readings into our lessons as questions arise about Alexie's humor, negative stereotypes, and moral consequences. Then we introduce students to the critical concept of "taking a stance" by discussing disagreements among critics' points of view on Alexie's work. We point out the conversational aspect of these pieces by highlighting the ways in which these critics speak to and speak back to each other. We ask students to join the conversation by writing "position papers," through which they speak to or speak back to Alexie's use of humor or negative stereotypes, or offer their thoughts on the moral implications of his work. Our prompt states:

> Drawing from your critical reader and writer's journal, sift through the impressions you have had of Alexie's work and find a question or reaction that you might want to investigate further. Reread the text and your response a few times. What do your questions and reactions tell you about your stance on the issue? If Alexie or any of these critics were in the room, what questions might you want to raise? How might they re-

spond? What position do you take on the issue? Would Alexie and/or the critics agree or disagree with you? In what ways? How might you explain your stance to him? What would you want to be sure to say? What do you want to add to the conversation?

For example, Elsie, a Blackfeet student, wrote about her dislike of Alexie's use of cuss words. Her family does not allow any profanity, so Alexie's frequent use of expletives made it impossible for her to find any moral redemption about Indian people in his stories and poems even though she liked reading about Indians today. Jason, a young man who lives on a ranch, took a similar stance: "I've never been assigned a book that took the Lord Jesus Christ's name in vain. I couldn't read after that." Casey, a non-Indian woman in an urban school, wrote that Alexie's use of humor and negative stereotypes helped her care about the plight of Indian people today, enough to want to write a letter to her legislators about making significant changes in Indian policy. These position papers give students the opportunity to take a critical stance on Alexie, to formulate positions related to the reading and to Alexie's representations of contemporary Native America that trouble their own preconceived perceptions of Indians in America today.

We also like to share some of Alexie's nonfiction to reinforce the significance of taking a critical stance. Alexie, a prolific essayist, is not short on outspoken opinions. He expertly models taking a critical stance on numerous topics, which helps students as they write critical opinions of their own.[1] We ask students to write a review, an opinion/editorial piece, or a letter to the editor of the local newspaper in which they revise their position paper in a new genre for a different audience. Here is an excerpt from a student letter published in our local paper:

Keep Prayer Out of Classroom

. . . I'm now attending high school and I feel that we shouldn't pray in school. I understand that people will raise their children how they want, but that may not be the way other people raise their children. I can say that if we started to pray in school, things wouldn't change.

Just because people pray doesn't make them perfect. People will always lie and hurt each other's feelings. Praying isn't the answer. Right now in my school, we are having a major issue with racism. I can guarantee that prayer wouldn't help the situation.

The way that people feel is the answer. If we can have this much hate over race, what do you think would happen to the people who prayed in front of the people who didn't feel that way? It would cause more pain than love, and it just doesn't need to happen. Kids these days in high school are very judgmental of the way people believe and what color their skin is.

This isn't a hate letter against God; this is the truth as I see it as a high school student, if we mandated prayer in schools. (Bell)

By practicing taking a critical stance, joining the conversation, and revising for a wider audience, students begin to appreciate firsthand what Alexie seems to be saying about the need for both Indians and non-Indians to examine the situation of Native Americans today and to work for redemption and the end to colonial oppression: "This is not a silent movie. Our voices will change our lives" ("Reservation Drive In," *First Indian on the Moon* 17).

Note

1. Much of Alexie's published nonfiction commentary is available through links on his website (http://www.fallsapart.com/essays.html). We recommend the material published in *Time* and the *Los Angeles Times* as most suitable to classroom use.

7 Flight and The Absolutely True Diary of a Part-Time Indian: Post-9/11 Hope and Reconciliation

■ ■

Since publication of the short story collection *The Toughest Indian in the World* (2000), Alexie's work has focused primarily on tensions between whites and Indians in intimate relationships, and between urban Indians and Indians still on the reservation. He told *Atlantic Unbound*'s Jessica Chapel, "Sixty percent of all Indians live in urban areas, but nobody's writing about them. They're really an underrepresented population" (par. 5–6). The dark novel *Indian Killer* is set in Seattle. Most of the stories in *Ten Little Indians* also take place in contemporary urban settings. Alexie's tone—though razor-sharp and still angry—has softened some and is more optimistic and hopeful than in earlier work. "Certainly I'm angry at the way Indians have been treated and continue to be treated. But I don't think it's a helpless emotion," he says (qtd. in Mabrey par. 9–12).

In his most recent novels, *Flight* and *The Absolutely True Diary of a Part-Time Indian*, Alexie attempts "to widen his embrace of the world and all the tribes in it" (Williams E11). Whereas Alexie's earlier work was the outcome of "Anger × Imagination," his maturing work draws on "expanded notions of tribalism, sympathetic biracial characters and empathic excursions into the minds of both victims and victimizers" rather than, for example, the "race-based rage" of his second novel, *Indian Killer* (Williams E11). Alexie says,

> [The terrorist attacks of September 11, 2001,] changed me tre-mendously. I saw the end game of tribalism—it ends up with people flying planes into buildings. I've worked hard since then to shed the negative parts of tribal thinking, which almost al-ways involve some sort of fear, the starting point for violence. *Indian Killer* is very much a tribal and fundamentalist book. I've really disowned it. (qtd. in Williams E11)

Readers can see Alexie struggling with these themes in *Diary*, which features Arnold Spirit, a.k.a. Junior, a fourteen-year-old re-cre-ation of Alexie during ninth grade in all-white Reardan High School "where he was the only Indian, except for the mascot" (*Diary* 56), and in *Flight*, which features a "young, edgy[,] outcast[,]" half-Irish, half-American Indian fifteen-year-old named Zits, who is "on the verge of colossal violence" (S. K. Walsh par. 1).

In the new novels, Alexie holds on to positive aspects of trib-alism in demonstrating his sense of belonging to certain commu-nities, of which his *Diary* protagonist, Junior, writes:

> I realized that, sure, I was a Spokane Indian. I belonged to that tribe. But I also belonged to the tribe of basketball players . . . bookworms . . . small-town kids . . . poverty . . . boys who really missed their best friends. (217)

Alexie also is questioning and "trying to understand what drives people to acts of both goodness and violence," a theme he ad-dresses head-on in *Flight*. "Set against massive acts of violence like 9/11, it's the small stories of betrayal and decency, of making the right choice or the wrong one, that interest Alexie" (Giese par. 3).

Both *Flight* and *Diary*—though painful and laced with Alexie's typical ribald humor, profanity, tragedy, alcoholism, sexual content, racist anecdotes, and violence—offer much that teachers might wish to consider with high school students. These aspects of the twenty-first century are a part of the world in which our students live. As Holmes stresses, educators cannot and should not try to keep the "real world" out of our classrooms, as some have tried to do in response to school violence. Like Holmes, we advocate reading *Flight* and *Diary* through a lens of critical inquiry that helps students to address actively with Alexie ways to make choices that rest on the side of peace and good.

Overview and Rationale

Flight

In his first novel since *Indian Killer* (1996), Alexie embarks on a journey to understand violence. He struggles with moral complexities and explores the ways in which "violence is perpetuated on both sides of any conflict and results in incredible acts of pain and suffering." He attempts to examine the question "Why does this keep happening?" (qtd. in Roberts). In *Flight*, Alexie's main character, introduced with an opening line that somewhat less spectacularly invokes the most famous in American literature— "Call me Zits. Everybody calls me Zits. . . . My real name isn't important."—is not off on "a perilous hunt for a great white whale . . . but a voyage of an entirely different dimension" (S. Kirk Walsh par. 3). Called so because he's afflicted with severe acne, Zits is essentially an orphan; his father left him at birth and his mother died of breast cancer when he was six. By the time the reader meets him, Zits has lived in twenty different foster homes and attended twenty-two different schools. His "entire life fits into one small backpack" (*Flight* 7).

Even though he comes across as an unlikable, alienating, and obnoxious kid, Zits's struggles with self-worth persuade readers to care about him:

> I'm dying from about ninety-nine kinds of shame. I'm ashamed of being fifteen years old. And being tall. And skinny. And ugly. I'm ashamed that I look like a bag of zits tied to a broomstick. I wonder if loneliness causes acne. I wonder if being Indian causes acne. (4)

Zits keeps running away from his foster homes and has many clashes with the police. After he lands in juvenile hall for the umpteenth time, he meets a young, white, "pretty-boy" anarchist named Justice, who teaches him how to take his sorry life into his own hands (S. K. Walsh). Justice advises Zits "to pray and then teaches him how to kill—and be killed" (Barbash par. 2).

During a shooting spree during which they brandish paintball and real guns in a bank, Zits is shot in the head by a security guard, whereupon he is catapulted through time like Billy Pilgrim in Kurt Vonnegut's *Slaughterhouse-Five* (Roberts). Zits resurfaces as a racist FBI agent heading toward a 1975 meeting with two prominent American Indian Movement (AIM) activists at Red River, Idaho; then as a mute Indian boy at the Battle of Little Bighorn moments before Custer arrives; then as Augustus (Gus) Sullivan, an aging Indian tracker employed by the U.S. Army during the Custer era. Falling through a series of nightmarish reincarnations in the bodies of others, including that of his alcoholic father, Zits survives his journey "through time and place and person and war" (*Flight* 108). Throughout his journeys, Zits struggles with stereotypes, self-identity, cultural identity, and abandonment. This boy is lonely, disappointed, scared, angry, and unsure. He does and says terrible things. Between the lines, he clearly longs to be loved; the violence he both enacts and witnesses is tied to that longing, and who can blame him? But Zits is also horrified by the evil he sees humans capable of, which leads to his redemption.

In Zits, Alexie has created an unlikely protagonist, an anti-hero—a self-absorbed, narcissistic fifteen-year-old boy whose mocking tone brings to mind a twenty-first-century Holden Caulfield and who, like his literary forebear, pretends not to care about anything. Some of the events depicted are visceral—brutal, gruesome, graphic, violent, and disturbing; Alexie delivers savage imagery with no remorse. But ultimately Zits is transformed in unexpected ways and leaves us on a note of hope. Zits thinks, as his new, soon-to-be-permanent foster mother hugs him, "I'm happy. I'm scared, too. I mean, I know the world is still a cold and cruel place. . . . But I'm beginning to think I've been given a chance. I'm beginning to think I might get unlonely" (180).

There is no question that *Flight* is a violent book. It is also a text interested in exploring our country's relationship to violence, and there is no way such a book could exist in any violence-free version. The ugly scenes nudge readers to confront horrific events in our past as well as reincarnations of them in the present. The subject of the book necessitates its story lines. Nonetheless, *Flight* is not *only* a violent book. Some of the most interesting work Alexie does with the text is highlighting the importance of small acts of decency: "'Go,' I say. 'Please.' It's the *please* that does it. Funny how a little politeness can change people's minds" (105). He reminds readers of our inability to ever know all sides of a story. With each experience Zits has, the more ambiguous become any causes or justifications for war. At one point, Zits discovers, "Art and Justice fight on opposite sides of the war but they sound exactly like each other. How can you tell the difference between the good and bad guys when they say exactly the same things?" (56). Once Zits begins to see things from other perspectives, he becomes unsure about everyone's actions and intentions, including his own: "Man I had no idea I was this evil. And then it makes me wonder. Do evil people *know* they're evil? Or do they just think they're doing the right thing?" (38). Many violent acts are committed (especially in the historical situations Alexie introduces) because the people involved believe they are doing the right thing, that they are making the world better. It is more difficult to rationalize violent acts when uncertain of intent than when convinced the actor intends to work for good, as in claims generally used to justify war.

Alexie unhinges Zits from time and place, from given notions of culture and identity, creating multiple possibilities for new cultural formations—for behaviors that open up possibilities other than violence as a response to humiliation, abandonment, and alienation. He foregrounds people's agency in sustaining and transforming constructions often deemed immutable—community, poverty, culture, identity, alcoholism.

On the one hand, we suspect teachers might find risky the idea of teaching a novel that deals so intimately with violence and that contains graphic language and sexual themes. However, Alexie does not do so gratuitously. The larger messages he sends speak more loudly than the complex tragedies he depicts. Ultimately, acts of humanity and kindness prevail in a violent world, which is why we think the novel holds promise for the classroom. On the other hand, some may rationalize teaching this book because they don't believe the violence will faze teens, that it's not any worse than anything students are surrounded by every day. If students are unfazed, however, this seems a much larger problem. Violence *does* matter. We shouldn't dismiss it as more of the same or simply more examples of that which our students see and hear every day. Instead we should lead students to think about the impact of such callousness on our society. Where are we headed if violence is the only communal practice we have left?

If we choose to read the book with students, it's partially because we hope it's not too late for them to be disturbed by the violence. The other thing *Flight* does is to remind us that individuals can influence history for the better. Small acts do make a difference; really, they contain our only power to influence larger acts of violence. Students need to contemplate that this is not an insignificant power. The day-to-day choices of individuals, how we choose to interact with others, what we model for those younger than ourselves, are important. Violence is not like natural disasters; it is preventable and it is something humans can control. The more people remember this and begin to act on it, the more significant change can be. Alexie helps readers see that violence is not the answer; peace is a more reasonable way.

An excellent reading and discussion guide that points readers to many of these themes and issues accompanies the Black Cat edition of the novel. Further readings are also recommended. Teachers will find this guide extremely useful in planning to read *Flight* with students; we do not think we can improve on those discussion suggestions here.

The Absolutely True Diary of a Part-Time Indian

The Absolutely True Diary of a Part-Time Indian is Alexie's 2007 National Book Award–winning young adult novel, and it is far less dark than *Flight*. *Diary*'s main character, who explores Indian identity both self and tribal, is a Spokane Indian boy from Wellpinit, Washington. Arnold Spirit, as he is known at Reardan High School (it's Junior at home on the reservation), is a bright fourteen-year-old, born with "water on the brain," who lives with several resultant maladies—oversized head; ten too many teeth; one eye that's far-sighted, the other near-sighted, requiring Coke-bottle glasses for correction—and endures a constant barrage of name-calling and bullying. Arnold prefers reading and drawing cartoons to the taunts he suffers outside his house. He says, "I draw because I feel like it may be my only real chance to escape the reservation. I think the world is a series of broken dams and floods, and my cartoons are tiny little lifeboats" (6). *Diary*, we should note, is vibrantly illustrated with art by Seattle artist Ellen Forney, whose depictions of the protagonist's cartoons are characters in themselves. Junior's only friend is a tough-guy named Rowdy, who protects Junior from his ever-present tormenters.

Readers who have examined Alexie's biographical information in Chapter 1 will instantly recognize the characteristics that Arnold/Junior shares with the author. As did Alexie, Junior takes the epic leap to transfer from the reservation school to the "rich, white" school in Reardan, twenty-two miles away from the rez, which Junior describes "is located approximately one million miles north of Important and two billion miles west of Happy" (3), in order to get a good education after he finds his mother's name in one of his textbooks. Things get complicated for Arnold/Junior when he goes to Reardan. At first he's an outcast, but he was an outcast at home, too. Soon he finds himself making friends at Reardan with both geeky and popular students and starting on the basketball team. When he plays basketball against Wellpinit, his whole tribe, including Rowdy, turns against him. During the course of the novel, Junior suffers the deaths of his beloved dog Oscar because the family is too poor to take him to the vet; of his grandmother, who is killed by a drunk driver; of his "uncle" Eugene, who is shot to death in a drunken assault by one of Eugene's good friends; and of his older sister, who dies in a house fire alongside her husband, both of them drunk and passed out. As Chris Shoemaker writes about *Diary*:

> The daily struggles of reservation life and [these] tragic deaths . . . would be all but unbearable without the humor and resilience of spirit with which Junior faces the world. The many characters, on and off the rez, with whom he has dealings are portrayed with compassion and verve, particularly the adults in his extended family. The teen's determination to both improve himself and overcome poverty, despite the handicaps of birth, circumstances, and race, delivers a positive message in a low-key manner. (*School Library Journal* par. 1)

In *Diary*, Alexie tells the story of an Indian teenager's identity crisis, which is his own story, and of how he works through it living in two worlds. The author brilliantly portrays the acceptance and the biases found in both societies. Alexie's *Diary* is endearing, tragic, deeply sad, and hilarious. As one reviewer said, "a more pedestrian writer" could never have pulled it off.

As with Zits in *Flight*, reviewers have celebrated the plights and persona of Arnold "Junior" Spirit as comparable to those of Holden Caulfield. Conversely, *Diary* has come under attack by some who question its appropriateness for use in school because of its profanity, homophobia, sexual references to masturbation and "getting into a girl's panties," an offensive racial joke that caused some students in an Illinois high school to walk out when Alexie read it from the book, and the prevalence of death from alcohol consumption. Many of our high school students live on an Indian reservation. They have read the book both independently and in literature circle groups; they love it. They love the voice. They find Arnold/Junior "realistic and authentic." We asked

Kelsey, who lived in Boston last year and has firsthand understanding of what people elsewhere think and don't know about Indians and reservations, what she thought about the book: "My mom thought the 'escape' message was too simple. I think it was the strongest message in the story and a realistic choice for Junior." We also asked her if she had any advice for teachers and readers off the rez, to which she responded:

> People might think the only thing on the rez is the negative stuff. Some of the most poignant moments in the book for me were those negative stories because they are so true; I have experienced this in my own life. Some people will read this and just laugh all the way through at the humor. They should realize this is the truth, it's autobiographical, not just funny.

Junior's remarkable ability to weather even the worst personal storms makes this an uplifting yet very emotional reading experience. The simple pencil cartoons by Seattle artist Ellen Forney fit perfectly within the story and reflect the burgeoning artist within Junior: "Reluctant readers can even skim the pictures and construct their own story based exclusively on Forney's illustrations" (Shoemaker, *SCL* par. 1); "they add a further, descriptive dimension to Junior's persona and are a great accompaniment to Alexie's forthright words and dramatic incidents" (Shoemaker, Amazon par. 3).

A reviewer at Teenreads reports

> It's an emotionally raw book, no question. My copy says 14 and up, and I might agree there. I might not buy it for my son's K–8 library, but I will recommend it to high school students and teachers. It is a painfully honest, clear-eyed, yet entertaining account of overcoming obstacles and learning to live with an identity both problematic and precious. (Siciliano par. 1–2)

As with *Flight*, teaching *The Absolutely True Diary of a Part-Time Indian* is not for the faint of heart. According to one reviewer:

> Unfortunately, there is a slim chance that [Alexie's] memorable work will ever find itself on the shelves of school libraries and into the hands of young adult readers without major abridgement. Many of the themes and a good deal of the language do not fit with standard considerations of what is considered appropriate reading material for young adult readers however wonderful and true-to-life the book is. (Mr. Techno par. 2)

We hope this isn't the case and provide ideas for teaching both *Flight* and *Diary* in conjunction with each other or separately.[1] We would point readers to Matt Berman's review and cautions at the Common Sense website and Janice Harayda's online review and "absolutely unauthorized" discussion questions at One-Minute Book Reviews for guiding young adult readers through the book. Readers can also hear Sherman Alexie read from *Diary* at www.lb-teens.com, which also has reviews of the book, and check out a list of the honors it has received (http://www.hachettebook groupusa.com/books/73/0316013684/index.html).

Themes and Proposed Activities

Finding One's Place

In both *Diary* and *Flight*, the main characters are struggling with a universal problem of adolescence: finding their own identity. They have discovered that there are different ways to label oneself and to be labeled by others, but both are troubled by trying to figure out what this means for them. Both stories explore how community identity and sense of belonging shape who one becomes and how one acts in the world. In *Diary*, Arnold/Junior is torn between two lives, the reservation life he knows and the outside world that he thinks he might want to be a part of. His friends at home call him "an apple" because he is "red on the outside and white on the inside" (132), and he too seems to believe there is some mismatch between how he looks and how he is expected to act. In *Flight*, Zits isn't torn between worlds; he feels he is a complete outsider to all of them. Or, as he says, he has "been partially raised by too many people" (6). He hasn't figured out how to be happy or successful anywhere.

Arnold/Junior says that all the time he was traveling between his home on the reservation and school in Reardan he "always felt like a stranger" (118). Before students read either book, it is helpful for them to begin thinking about one of the primary themes in both: identity conflicts. To stimulate ideas, we examine one of Ellen Forney's illustrations from *Diary*, a picture of Arnold/Junior with a line drawn down the middle of his body. The left side is labeled "white" and drawn and labeled with "appropriate" characteristics. The left side is labeled "Indian" (57). We ask students to respond by drawing their own versions, with themselves as subjects, thinking about what areas of their life might feel split in similar ways. Their images might illustrate racial, cultural, geographic, or religious differences, or differences in personal characteristics such as that of "half obedient child" and "half rebellious teenager." They might split their drawings in more than two ways. From this exercise, students can be prompted to freewrite about what it feels like to "walk in two or more worlds" at once: "How do these identities synchronize, clash, or something else? How do these differences impact decision making, such as deciding what is the right or wrong thing to do?" Many of our students are visual learners (like Junior) and often have more to write about if they can start with an exercise like this. Modeling Forney's labeling of everything is a technique to suggest for students not confident in their drawing abilities. They can include any important details regardless of whether they think they can draw.

In *Flight*, Zits struggles with identity by dissociating. Like Arnold/Junior, he has trouble fitting in, but not because his worlds are in conflict. He doesn't see himself as belonging in any of the places he goes or with any of the people he meets. He begins to create an identity for himself by eliminating what he doesn't want to be rather than by emulating others he respects. You might extend the drawing/writing activity by asking students whether they've ever felt as Zits does. Are there any places where or times when they couldn't figure out who they were or how they wanted to act? Which situations or groups have they found themselves in through circumstances they may not have been able to control or that didn't seem to make sense? How did they respond?

Playing by the Rules

Finding one's place is not just a matter of following society's rules; we first must learn the rules and understand when and how to apply them. Once we are immersed in a culture, we tend to take all the rules we know for granted, but if we are thrown into a new situation it can be nearly impossible to figure out what is expected. Both Zits and Arnold/Junior struggle with not knowing "the rules."

Diary

After reading the chapter "How to Fight Off Monsters," students will find it natural to discuss the idea of the rules people live by. When Junior leaves the reservation, the rules he knows for interacting with others no longer apply, yet following the "unofficial and unwritten" rules of any community is vital to an individual's survival. These are the rules that people notice only when they are out of place; in our area, for example, we always wave when passing someone while driving on a gravel road. To not wave is to invite a look at your license plate to find out where you—the obvious stranger—are from. Ask students to think about the routine ways they interact with others every day, such as riding on the bus, walking in a mall, passing people in a hallway, or standing in an elevator. What are the unwritten rules they live by? Pair students up and have them discuss these rules. Then open up the issue to whole-group discussion to take it a step deeper, if possible. Alexie is concerned with cultural differences. If your class is able, have them discuss cultural "rules"; it might be easier for them to notice things about cultures other than their own. This exercise could evolve into a poem or other writing assignment that illuminates students' beliefs and ideas about themselves as well as others.

Flight

Zits has the same problem as Arnold/Junior; he isn't familiar with the little details about how to act if he wants to fit into mainstream society, which seems to be the goal with most of his foster home placements. In the chapter "Small Ceremonies," Zits's social worker summarizes his problem by concluding that he has "never developed a sense of citizenship." According to her, "It's all in the small ceremonies" (5–6). Zits is unfamiliar with little behaviors such as wearing shined shoes and a necktie on more formal occasions. Students might consider the small ceremonies that are expected in groups to which they belong. What behaviors indicate to those around them that they belong? Discussion prompts might include "Do you know how to tie a tie? Shoot a basketball? Load songs on an iPod? Drive a stick-shift car? Milk a cow? Read a subway map? Sail a boat?" All groups, be they cultural, religious, geographic, socioeconomic, or age-specific, engage in specific ceremonies. What groups do students participate in, and what ceremonies performed by those groups indicate membership?

Seeing through Another's Eyes

In both texts, Alexie seems interested in raising the question of how perspective, knowledge, and community beliefs can dramatically change how we view an experience. Some of the events in each book would be dramatically different if told from another character's point of view. Alexie challenges readers to consider how experience influences which side of an argument we take or how we interpret things. We might ask students to extend this idea by trying to imagine from an alternate point of view some of the events Alexie describes. Students might team with a partner and then choose an event to rewrite from a different character's point of view. How might this new character's experience change the story that is reported? What about background knowledge? How might the voice differ? After students have rewritten the telling of the event, they might share with the class and gather feedback about how realistic their version seems. Discuss how the manner of telling influences what is told or what is recorded as official history. Both *Flight* and *Diary* contain possible sections for revisionist writing.

Flight

Students might rewrite any of Zits's clashes with his foster families or the law from others' points of view. Students might also work with the different chunks of history Zits experiences as a way to take yet another look at the events and recorded historical facts to see in what other ways the events might be interpreted. In

Chapters 4 through 6, Zits is FBI agent Hank Storm in the middle of Red River, Idaho, on the Nannapush Reservation in 1975; the story would be much different told through the eyes of his partner, Elk, Horse, or Hank's wife. In Chapters 7 through 9, Zits is a young Native boy who hears from a distance the Battle of the Little Bighorn in June 1876; Crazy Horse, Sitting Bull, General George Armstrong Custer, or any of the soldiers on either side would have alternate views of this event. In Chapters 10 through 12, Zits is Augustus Sullivan, a successful Indian tracker; how might his story differ if told from the point of view of the "cruel and impulsive" "kid" soldiers (82), General Mustache (Custer), Bow Boy, Small Saint, or the girl in the gingham dress? In Chapters 13 through 15, Zits is Jimmy, an airplane flight instructor who taught a Muslim terrorist how to fly; how might the story be told by Abbad, Jimmy's wife, his girlfriend Helda, or the newscasters covering the plane hijacking or Jimmy's final flight? In Chapters 16 through 18, Zits is his father; what might Zits or his mother have to say to him?

Diary

This novel also offers opportunities for students to explore perspective. Junior's experiences at Reardan High School constitute the main conflict of the book and are spread throughout most of the novel, but students can still pick one character and have him or her talk about events from his or her point of view. Rowdy, for instance, doesn't get to tell us his side of the story. And what do Junior's parents, grandmother, and sister really think about his request to attend Reardan? How might their interior monologues sound? What about the other people on the reservation? What about Roger? Penelope? Gordy?

After Junior's conflict with Mr. P, his geography teacher, Junior accidentally breaks Mr. P's nose when he throws a book. Mr. P eventually apologizes to Junior for every awful thing he's done to other Indian kids in the past. These apologies include being sorry for following the "Kill the Indian to save the child" instruction he was told to implement. Mr. P urges Junior to get away, to leave the reservation forever, because everyone there is "defeated" (42). Students might write from the perspective of Mr. P or that of some of the students he mistreated. They might research Indian boarding schools such as Haskell and Carlisle, where "Kill the Indian to save the child" was the accepted pedagogical practice, and write from the point of view of one of those students.

Junior also writes in his diary about his sister Mary's "escape" to Montana. Readers know she wanted to be a romance writer but just seemed to lose all ambition after high school: "After seven years of living in the basement and watching TV, after doing absolutely nothing at all, my sister decided she needed to change her life" by getting married and moving away (89). Although Mary sends an email and a postcard, we don't see the story from her point of view. Alexie has written a great deal about the house fire and deaths of his sister Mary and her husband. It might be provocative to compare the story of Mary's tragic death in *Diary* with Alexie's portrayals in the "Sister Fire, Brother Smoke" poems in *The Summer of Black Widows* (49–62) and the poems "Fire Storm" (23–28) and "House(fires)" (45–48) from *First Indian on the Moon*.

Moving beyond Tribalism
Both *Flight* and *Diary* represent a shift away from tribalism in the traditional sense. In these texts, tribal associations shape individuals, but both protagonists also discover they are more than

their tribal identity and that sometimes being Indian isn't enough to bind two Native people together. After trying to recognize himself in the band of Indians who have just slaughtered some white women and children, Zits concludes, "we're not all the same kind of Indians, are we?" (87). In *Diary*, Junior's words sound like they could be from an interview with Alexie: "I used to think the world was broken down by tribes . . . but now I know that isn't true. The world is only broken into two tribes: The people who are assholes and the people who are not" (176). Junior continues to struggle with where he fits into his tribe and, ultimately he concludes that he is not only a member of the Spokane tribe but also a member of at least fourteen other "tribes," everything from "the tribe of cartoonists" to the "tribe of small town kids." He discovers, "I was not alone in my loneliness. There were millions of other Americans who had left their birthplaces in search of a dream" (217). He begins to become more optimistic when he realizes there are many other ways to belong and connect with others. After rereading with students Junior's list of tribal memberships, have them write their own lists. In what different groups can they claim membership? After they've developed their lists, they might think about the benefits of belonging to more, rather than fewer, "tribes."

Keeping in mind Junior's realization that "[i]f you let people into your life a little bit, they can be pretty damn amazing" (129), a realization that Zits also comes to at the end of *Flight*, challenge students to pair up with someone in the class they know little about. The smaller the school, the more difficult this task will be, but even in the tiniest towns, not everyone really knows everything about everyone (even if they think they do). Challenge the class to see which pair can come up with the longest list of things they have in common in three minutes. After students complete their list and have had time to share briefly with the class some interesting discoveries, ask them to take the task a step further by creating a paragraph-length character sketch about their partner. Let them work on this with their partner so they can ask additional questions and add details to their piece. If both the author and the subject feel comfortable, share a few of the pieces in teams or with the entire class.

Understanding, Reconciliation, Responsibility

We are accustomed to hearing angry comments from other teachers and our students while teaching the works of Sherman Alexie. In our experience in Montana, such comments often include statements such as "I never killed an Indian. I'm not responsible for the way Indians live today." A well-intentioned person might indeed be stating the truth of the first proposition; the second claim, however, requires a second look if teachers want to do antiracist work—to do more than examine stereotypes and the negative aspects of tribalism explored in Alexie's novels.

Although none of us may have directly participated in Indian genocide or ongoing acts of violence toward Indian peoples, all non–Native Americans have benefited and continue to benefit from our country's legacy of removal and holocaust. The land we live on once supported millions of Native people. Indian people were forcibly removed, starved to death, and killed by the scores so that Euro-Americans and others could move in and enjoy the benefits of American abundance. Whether or not we lived here during the times of the Indian wars and confinement to reservations is irrelevant. The fact that the land was "opened to discovery" by multiple acts of violence is a legacy from which every non–Native American resident benefits. To teach Alexie's work is to agree to do antiracist work, to try to understand this violent legacy, to work for reconciliation toward Indian peoples. In doing so, we must take responsibility—we must "own up" to the facts of American history. We must acknowledge the benefits we receive as a result of a genocidal legacy: land ownership, freedom to come and go as we please on a vast continent, access to higher-quality education and jobs—and these are just a few examples. Though we may have worked hard to earn what we have, we also must realize that we, as privileged inheritors of a legacy that continues to oppress Indian peoples, have a responsibility to work for justice and equity by *noticing* injustice and inequity and working to undo it where we are able. "Owning up" means responding in whatever arenas of influence our privilege allows us to enjoy—through work in schools, churches, synagogues, community memberships—to notice anti-Indian racism, to do our homework and find out the facts, to stop perpetuating the myths and stereotypes, and to offer correctives. To speak the truth to power with love (Freire; hooks) wherever and whenever we are able. This is what it means to take responsibility.

"Democracy needs her poets, in all their diversity, precisely because our hope for survival is in recognizing the reality of one another's lives," writes Bill Moyers in *The Language of Life: A Festival of Poets* (xi). Examining the difficult issues raised by Alexie in ways that allow his words to change our hearts about the negative effects of tribalism and the sorry outcomes of violence and rage helps give both our students and us spaces and opportunities to speak and to hear a more commodious language, language that makes room for our students' anecdotal, personal, and cultural reflections as well as the reflections of those different from themselves. Our intent, as Jim Corder has counseled, is to speak a commodious language, creating a world full of space and time that will hold our diversities. Most failures of communication result from some willful or inadvertent but unloving violation of the space and time we and others live in, and most of our speaking is tribal talk. But there is more to us than that. We can learn to speak a commodious language, and we can learn to hear a commodious language. (189)

Sherman Alexie helps us find more ways to teach for peace.

Note

1. Because *Flight* and *Diary* are such recent publications, we have not yet field-tested these ideas. We offer speculative thinking based on our students' responses so far to reading the books primarily on their own.

Works by Sherman Alexie

■ ■

Poetry

The Business of Fancydancing: Stories and Poems. Brooklyn, NY: Hanging Loose Press, 1992.

Old Shirts and New Skins. Los Angeles: American Indian Studies Center, University of California, Los Angeles, 1993.

First Indian on the Moon. Brooklyn, NY: Hanging Loose Press, 1993.

The Summer of Black Widows. Brooklyn, NY: Hanging Loose Press, 1996.

One Stick Song. Brooklyn, NY: Hanging Loose Press, 2000.

Limited Edition Chapbooks

I Would Steal Horses. Niagara Falls, NY: Slipstream Press, 1992.

Seven Mourning Songs for the Cedar Flute I Have Yet to Learn to Play. Spokane: Whitman College Book Arts Press, 1994.

Water Flowing Home. Boise, ID: Limberlost Press, 1996.

The Man Who Loves Salmon. Boise, ID: Limberlost Press, 1998.

Dangerous Astronomy. Boise, ID: Limberlost Press, 2005.

Wicazo Sa Review

"In Response to Elizabeth Cook-Lynn's Pronouncement That I One of the New, Angry (Warriors) Kind of Like Norman Schwarzkopf and Rush Limbaugh." *Wicazo Sa Review* 9.2 (Autumn 1993): 9.

Short Story Collections

The Lone Ranger and Tonto Fistfight in Heaven. New York: Atlantic Monthly Press, 1993.

The Toughest Indian in the World. New York: Atlantic Monthly Press, 2000.

Ten Little Indians. New York: Grove Press, 2003.

Novels

Reservation Blues. New York: Atlantic Monthly Press, 1995.

Indian Killer. New York: Atlantic Monthly Press, 1996.

Flight. New York: Black Cat, 2007.

Young Adult Novels

The Absolutely True Diary of a Part-Time Indian. Boston: Little, Brown, 2007.

Screenplays

Smoke Signals: The Screenplay. Hyperion, 1998.

The Business of Fancydancing: The Screenplay. Brooklyn, NY: Hanging Loose Press, 2003.

Selected Essays

"Superman and Me." *Los Angeles Times* 19 April 1998. 26 Feb. 2008 <http://www.fallsapart.com/superman.html>.

"I Hated Tonto (Still Do)." *Los Angeles Times* 28 June 1998. 26 Feb. 2008 <http://www.fallsapart.com/tonto.html>.

"Some of My Best Friends." Rev. of Ian Frazier's *On The Rez. Los Angeles Times* 23 Jan. 2000. 26 Feb. 2008 <http://www.fallsapart.com/ontherez.html>.

"What Sacagawea Means to Me." *Time* 30 June 2002. 26 Feb. 2008 <http://www.time.com/time/2002/lewis_clark/lprocon.html>.

"When the Story Stolen Is Your Own." *Time* 29 Jan. 2006. 26 Feb. 2008 <http://www.time.com/time/magazine/article/0,9171,1154221,00.html>.

Official Website

shermanalexie.com. 25 Feb. 2008 <http://www.fallsapart.com>.

Bibliography

ATWELL, NANCIE. *Naming the World: A Year of Poems and Lessons.* Portsmouth, NH: Firsthand, 2006.

BARBASH, TOM. "Native Son" Rev. of *Flight,* by Sherman Alexie. *The New York Times* 27 May 2007. 1 Feb. 2008 <http://www.nytimes.com/2007/05/27/books/review/Barbash2-t.html?_r=1&oref=slogin>.

BARCOTT, BRUCE. "Off the Rez." Rev. of *The Absolutely True Diary of a Part-Time Indian,* by Sherman Alexie. *The New York Times* 11 Nov. 2007. 1 Feb. 2008 <http://www.nytimes.com/2007/11/11/books/review/Barcott3-t.html?_r=1&ref=authors&pagewanted=print&oref=slogin>.

BAXTER, ANDREA-BESS. Rev. of *Old Shirts and New Skins, First Indian on the Moon,* and *The Lone Ranger and Tonto Fistfight in Heaven,* by Sherman Alexie. *Western American Literature* 29.3 (1994). 277–80.

BELL, BRITNEE. "Keep Prayer Out of Classroom." Letter. *The Missoulian* 22 May 2007. <http://www.missoulian.com/articles/2007/05/22/letters/letters3.txt>.

BELLANTE, JOHN, AND CARL BELLANTE. Interview. "Sherman Alexie, Literary Rebel." *Bloomsbury Review* 14 (1994): 14–15, 26.

BERMAN, MATT. Rev. of *The Absolutely True Diary of a Part-Time Indian,* by Sherman Alexie. 1 Feb. 2008 <http://www.commonsensemedia.org/book-reviews/Absolutely-True-Diary-Part.html>.

BIGELOW, BILL, AND BOB PETERSON, EDS. *Rethinking Columbus: The Next 500 Years.* Milwaukee: Rethinking Schools, 1998.

BIRD, GLORIA. "The Exaggeration of Despair in Sherman Alexie's *Reservation Blues.*" *Wicazo Sa Review* 11.2 (1995): 47–52.

BISHOP, WENDY. *Thirteen Ways of Looking for a Poem: A Guide to Writing Poetry.* New York: Addison Wesley Longman, 2000.

BLAU, SHERIDAN D. *The Literature Workshop: Teaching Texts and Their Readers.* Portsmouth, NH: Heinemann, 2003.

BOMER, RANDY. *Time for Meaning: Crafting Literate Lives in Middle and High School.* Portsmouth, NH: Heinemann, 1995.

BOOTH, DAVID. *Story Drama: Creating Stories through Role Playing, Improvising, and Reading Aloud.* 2nd ed. Markham, Ontario: Pembroke, 2005.

BRILL, SUSAN BERRY DE RAMIREZ. "Sherman Alexie." *Native American Writers of the United States.* Dictionary of Literary Biography Ser. 175. Ed. Kenneth M. Roemer. Detroit: Gale Group, 1997. 3–10.

BRUCE, HEATHER E., AND BRYAN D. DAVIS. "Slam: Hip-hop Meets Poetry—A Strategy for Violence Intervention." *English Journal* 89.5 (2000): 119–27.

BURGOYNE, ROBERT. *Film Nation: Hollywood Looks at U.S. History.* Minneapolis: U of Minnesota P, 1997.

CAPRICCIOSO, ROBERT. "Sherman Alexie: American Indian Filmmaker/Writer Talks with Robert Capriccioso." 23 Mar. 2003. 16 Sept. 2007 <http://www.identitytheory.com/interviews/alexie_interview.html>.

CARNES, MARK C., ED. "Conversation between Mark Carnes and Oliver Stone." *Past Imperfect: History According to the Movies.* New York: Henry Holt, 1996.

CHAPEL, JESSICA. Interview with Sherman Alexie. *Atlantic Unbound.* 1 June 2000 <http://www.theatlantic.com/unbound/interviews/ba2000-06-01.htm.>

CHEUSE, ALAN. "Alexie's *Absolutely True Diary.*" Rev. on NPR's "All Things Considered." 1 Oct. 2007. 1 Feb. 2008 <http://www.npr.org/templates/story/story.php?storyId=14871881>.

CHRISTENSEN, LINDA. *Reading, Writing, and Rising Up: Teaching about Social Justice and the Power of the Written Word.* Milwaukee: Rethinking Schools, 2000.

CLINE, LYNN. "About Sherman Alexie." *Ploughshares* 26.4 (2000/2001): 197–202. 24 Jan. 2008 <http://www.pshares.org/issues/article.cfm?prmArticleID=5027>.

COOK-LYNN, ELIZABETH. "Who Gets to Tell the Stories?" *Wicazo Sa Review* 9.1 (1993): 60–64.

CORDER, JIM. "Argument as Emergence, Rhetoric as Love." *Selected Essays of Jim Corder: Pursuing the Personal in Scholarship, Teaching, and Writing.*

Ed. James S. Baumlin and Keith D. Miller. Urbana, IL: National Council of Teachers of English, 2004. 170–89.

COULOMBE, JOSEPH L. "The Approximate Size of His Favorite Humor: Sherman Alexie's Comic Connections and Disconnections in *The Lone Ranger and Tonto Fistfight in Heaven*." *American Indian Quarterly* 26.1 (2002): 94–115.

COX, JAMES. "Muting White Noise: The Subversion of Popular Culture Narratives in Sherman Alexie's Fiction." *Studies in American Indian Literature* 9.4 (1997): 52–70.

CROSSROADS. Dir. Walter Hill. Perf. Ralph Macchio, Joe Seneca, Jami Gertz, Joe Morton, Robert Judd. Sony, 1986.

CUMMINS, ANN. "Time-Traveling Boy: A Native American Orphan Finds a Way to Escape His Misery." Rev. of *Flight,* by Sherman Alexie. *The Washington Post* 15 April 2007. 1 Feb. 2008 <http://www.washington post.com/wp-dyn/content/article/2007/04/12/AR2007041202510. html>.

DAMERON, EVA. "From Rez Kid to Respected Author: Award-Winning Writer to Visit UNM and Discuss New Book." *The New Mexico Daily Lobo* 23 Oct. 2007. 1 Feb. 2008 <http://media.www.dailylobo.com/ media/storage/paper344/news/2007/10/23/Culture/From-Rez.Kid.To.Respected.Author-3050257.shtml>.

"A DIALOGUE ON RACE WITH PRESIDENT CLINTON." *The NewsHour with Jim Lehrer.* PBS. 9 July 1998. Transcript available at http://www.pbs.org/ newshour/bb/race_relations/OneAmerica/transcript.html.

DIMITRIADIS, GREG, AND CAMERON MCCARTHY. *Reading and Teaching the Postcolonial: From Baldwin to Basquiat and Beyond.* New York: Teachers College Press, 2001.

DIX, ANDREW. "Escape Stories: Narratives and Native Americans in Sherman Alexie's *The Lone Ranger and Tonto Fistfight in Heaven.*" Yearbook of English Studies. 31. *North American Short Stories and Short Fictions.* Ed. Nicola Bradbury. Leeds, UK: Maney-Modern Humanities Research Association, 2001. 155–67.

ELEVELD, MARK, ED. *The Spoken Word Revolution: Slam, Hip Hop & the Poetry of a New Generation.* Naperville, IL: Sourcebooks, 2003.

EVANS, STEPHEN F. "'Open Containers': Sherman Alexie's Drunken Indians." *American Indian Quarterly* 25.1 (2001): 46–72.

EVANS-LYNN, LORILEE. "Slammin'." *Montana Writing Project Journal* 1.4 (2007): 4–14. 16 Aug. 2007 <http://www.cas.umt.edu/english/mwp/ publications.html>.

FRASER, JOELLE. "An Interview with Sherman Alexie." *Iowa Review* 30.3 (2000): 59–70. 17 June 2005 <http://www.english.uiuc.edu/maps/ poets/a_f/alexie/fraser.htm>.

FRIERE, PAULO. *Pedagogy of the Oppressed.* New York: Seabury, 1970.

GIESE, RACHE. "Inner Conflict: Sherman Alexie's Soul-Searching New Novel." *CBC Arts/Books* 19 June 2007. 20 Sept. 2007 <http:// www.cbc.ca/arts/books/alexie.html>.

GILLAN, JENNIFER. "Reservation Home Movies: Sherman Alexie's Poetry." *American Literature* 68.1 (1996): 91–110.

GOEBEL, BRUCE A. *Reading Native American Literature: A Teacher's Guide.* Urbana, IL: National Council of Teachers of English, 2004.

GRAFF, GERALD. *Beyond the Culture Wars: How Teaching the Conflicts Can Revitalize American Education.* New York: Norton, 1992.

GRAFF, GERALD, AND JAMES PHELAN, EDS. *Mark Twain's* The Adventures of Huckleberry Finn: *Case Studies in Critical Controversy.* 2nd ed. Boston: Bedford/St. Martin's, 2004.

———. *William Shakespeare's* The Tempest: *Case Studies in Critical Controversy.* Boston: Bedford/St. Martin's, 2000.

GRANDE, SANDY. *Red Pedagogy: Native American Social and Political Thought.* Lanham, MD: Rowman & Littlefield, 2004.

GRASSIAN, DANIEL. *Understanding Sherman Alexie.* Columbia: U of South Carolina P, 2005.

HARAYDA, JANICE. Rev. of *The Absolutely True Diary of a Part-Time Indian,* by Sherman Alexie. 1 Jan. 2008. 1 Feb. 2008 <http://oneminutebook reviews.wordpress.com/2008/01/16/>.

HIGHWAY, TOMSON. "Spokane Words: Tomson Highway Raps with Sherman Alexie." *Aboriginal Voices* January–March 1997. 16 May 2008 <http:// www. fallsapart.com/art-av.html>.

HIMMELSBACH, ERIK. "The Reluctant Spokesman." Interviews. *Los Angeles Times* 17 Dec. 1996. 17 July 2005 <http://www.fallsapart.com/art-lat. html>.

HOLBROOK, SARA, AND MICHAEL SALINGER. *Outspoken! How to Improve Writing and Speaking Skills through Poetry Performance.* Portsmouth, NH: Heinemann, 2006.

HOLLRAH, PATRICE E. M. "'I'm Talking like a Twentieth-Century Indian Woman': Contemporary Female Warriors in the Works of Sherman Alexie." *"The Old Lady Trill, the Victory Yell": The Power of Women.* New York: Routledge, 2004: 133–70.

HOLMES, MARSHA LEE. "Get Real: Violence in Popular Culture *and* in English Class." *A Curriculum of Peace.* Ed. Virginia Monseau. Urbana, IL: National Council of Teachers of English, 2004. 122–32.

HOOKS, BELL. *Black Looks: Race and Representation.* Boston: South End Press, 1992.

"INDIAN LAWMAKERS ASSAIL COMMENTS ABOUT RESERVATIONS." *Missoulian.com News Online* 10 Mar. 2001. 11 Mar. 2002 <http://www.missoulian.com/archives/inde…etail&doc=/2001/march/10-230-news10.txt>.

IVRY, BOB. "From the Reservation of His Mind." *Bergen* [New Jersey] *Record* 28 June 1998. 24 Jan. 2008 <http://www.theangrypoet.com/archives/voice/alexie>.

KEELER, JACQUELINE. "Laughing at the Lone Ranger." *Colorlines* 1.3 (1999): 32–34.

KINCAID, JAMES R. "Who Gets to Tell Their Stories?" *New York Times Book Review* 3 May 1992: 24–29.

KRUPAT, ARNOLD. "The 'Rage Stage': Contextualizing Sherman Alexie's *Indian Killer.*" *Red Matters: Native American Studies.* Philadelphia: U of Pennsylvania P, 2002. 98–121.

LINCOLN, KENNETH. "Futuristic Hip Indian: Alexie." *Sing with the Heart of a Bear: Fusions of Native and American Poetry, 1890–1999.* Berkeley: U of California P, 2000. 267–74.

———. *Native American Renaissance.* Berkeley: U of California P, 1983.

LITSITE ALASKA. "Pictures and Words: Meeting Sherman Alexie." 26 Feb. 2008 <http://litsite.alaska.edu/aktraditions/nativepride/alexei.html>.

LOEWEN, JAMES W. *Lies My Teacher Told Me: Everything Your American History Textbook Got Wrong.* New York: Touchstone, 1995.

LOUIS, ADRIAN. Foreword. *Old Shirts and New Skins.* By Sherman Alexie. Los Angeles: American Indian Studies Center, University of California, 1993: vii–x.

Low, Denise. Rev. of *The Lone Ranger and Tonto Fistfight in Heaven*. *American Indian Quarterly* 20.1 (1996): 123.

Luce, Mark S. "*Flight* by Sherman Alexie: A Troubled Half-Native American Teen Goes Time-Traveling." Rev. *The Los Angeles Times* 8 April 2007. 1 Feb. 2008 <http://www.latimes.com/features/printedition/books/la-bk-luce8apr08,1,6572455,print.story?ctrack=3&cset=true>.

Lundquist, Suzanne Evertson. *Native American Literatures: An Introduction*. New York: Continuum, 2004.

Lyons, Scott Richard. "Rhetorical Sovereignty: What Do American Indians Want from Writing?" *College Composition and Communication* 51.3 (2000): 447–68.

Mabrey, Vicki. "The Toughest Indian in the World: An Interview with Sherman Alexie." *60 Minutes II*. CBS. WCBS, New York. 20 Mar. 2001. 28 Jan. 2008 <http://www.cbsnews.com/stories/2001/01/19/60II/main265512.shtml?source=search_story>.

McFarland, Ron. "Another Kind of Violence: Sherman Alexie's Poems." *American Indian Quarterly* 21.2 (1997): 251–64.

———. *Dictionary of Literary Biography*. 206. *Twentieth-Century American Western Writers, First Series*. Detroit: Gale Group, 1999. 3–10.

McLaughlin, Gary L. "The Way to Confusion." *English Journal* 86 (1997): 70–75.

McNally, Joel. "Sherman Alexie." *Writer* 114.6 (2001). 28–31.

Mihelich, John. "Smoke Signal? American Popular Culture and the Challenge to Hegemonic Images of American Indians in Native American Film." *Wicazo Sa Review* 16.2 (2001): 129–37.

Mihesuah, Devon A. *American Indians: Stereotypes & Realities*. Atlanta: Clarity, 1996.

Moore, David L. "Sherman Alexie: Irony, Intimacy, and Agency." *Cambridge Companion to Native American Literature*. Ed. Joy Porter and Kenneth M. Roemer. Cambridge, UK: Cambridge UP, 2005. 297–310.

Moyers, Bill. *The Language of Life: A Festival of Poets*. New York: Main Street Books, 1996.

"Mr. Techno." Rev. of *The Absolutely True Diary of a Part-Time Indian,* by Sherman Alexie. 3 Feb. 2008 <http://www.amazon.com/gp/pdp/profile/A1Q4LE9A6IVGOZ/ref=cm_cr_pr_pdp>.

NATIVELANDZ. "Sherman J. Alexie, Jr." 22 Nov. 2005. 23 Jan. 2008 <http://www.nativelandz.net/new/index.php?option=com_content&task=view&id=75&Itemid=39>.

NEALON, JEFFREY, AND SUSAN SEARLS GIROUX. *The Theory Toolbox: Critical Concepts for the Humanities, Arts, and Social Sciences.* Lanham, MD: Rowman & Littlefield, 2003.

NELSON, WILLIE. "My Heroes Have Always Been Cowboys." *The Essential Willie Nelson.* Columbia, 2003.

NYGREN, ASE. "A World of Story-Smoke: A Conversation with Sherman Alexie." Interview. *MELUS* 30.4 (2005): 149–69. 21 Jan. 2008 <http://www.thefreelibrary.com/A+world+of+story-smoke%3a+a+conversation+with+Sherman+Alexie.-a0140561634>.

O'CONNOR, JOHN. *Wordplaygrounds: Reading, Writing, and Performing Poetry in the English Classroom.* Urbana, IL: National Council of Teachers of English, 2004.

OWENS, LOUIS. "As If an Indian Were Really an Indian: Native American Voices and Postcolonial Theory." *Native American Representations: First Encounters, Distorted Images, and Literary Appropriations.* Ed. Gretchen M. Bataille. Lincoln: U of Nebraska P, 2001: 11–25.

———. *Other Destinies: Understanding the American Indian Novel.* Norman: U of Oklahoma P, 1992.

PABST, GEORGIA. "Alexie Sends Strong Signals: Writer Spares No One from Barbs." *Milwaukee Journal Sentinel* 9 March 2002. Sept. 2005 <http://www.jsonline.com/enter/books/mar02/25632.asp>.

PADGETT, RON. *The Teachers and Writers Handbook of Poetic Forms.* 2nd ed. New York: Teachers and Writers Collaborative, 2000.

PORTER, JOY. "Historical and Cultural Contexts to Native American Literature." *The Cambridge Companion to Native American Literature.* Ed. Joy Porter and Kenneth Roemer. Cambridge, UK: Cambridge U P, 2005. 39–68.

PORTER, JOY, AND KENNETH M. ROEMER, EDS. *The Cambridge Companion to Native American Literature.* Cambridge, UK: Cambridge U P, 2005.

QUIRK, SARAH A. *Dictionary of Literary Biography.* 278. *American Novelists since World War II, Seventh Series.* Detroit: Gale Group, 2003.

RAY, KATIE WOOD. *Wondrous Words: Writers and Writing in the Elementary School.* Urbana, IL: National Council of Teachers of English, 1999.

RICHTER, DAVID. *Falling into Theory: Conflicting Views on Reading Literature.* 2nd ed. Boston: Bedford/St. Martin's, 2000.

ROBERTS, REBECCA. "Sherman Alexie Talks *Flight.*" Interview. "Talk of the Nation," NPR. 11 Apr. 2007. 5 Sept. 2007 <http://www.npr.org/templates/story/story.php?storyId=9517855>.

ROEMER, KENNETH M. Introduction. *The Cambridge Companion to Native American Literature.* Cambridge, UK: Cambridge U P, 2005. 1–24.

———. Introduction. *Native American Writers of the United States.* Ed. Kenneth M. Roemer. Dictionary of Literary Biography Ser. 175. Detroit: Gale Group, 1997. xi–xxi.

———. "Timeline: Literary, Historical, and Cultural Conjunctions." *The Cambridge Companion to Native American Literature.* Cambridge, UK: Cambridge U P, 2005. 25–38.

RUOFF, A. LAVONNE BROWN. *American Indian Literatures: An Introduction, Bibliographic Review, and Selected Bibliography.* New York: Modern Language Association, 1990.

SAUCERMAN, JAMES R. "Teaching American Indian Literature." *Teaching American Indian Students.* Ed. Jon Reyhner. Norman: U of Oklahoma P, 1992. 192–208.

THE SEARCH FOR ROBERT JOHNSON. DVD. Dir. Chris Hunt. Perf. Jr. John Hammond. Sony Corporation, 1992.

SHOEMAKER, CHRIS. Rev. of *The Absolutely True Diary of a Part-Time Indian,* by Sherman Alexie. 1 Sept. 2007. 1 Feb. 2008 <http://www.school libraryjournal.com/index.asp?layout=articlePrint&articleID=CA6473870>.

———. Rev. of *The Absolutely True Diary of a Part-Time Indian,* by Sherman Alexie. 31 Jan. 2008 <http://www.amazon.com/exec/obidos/ASIN/0316013684/thebookreport01>.

SICILIANO, JANA. Rev. of *The Absolutely True Diary of a Part-Time Indian,* by Sherman Alexie. *Teenreads.* 31 Jan. 2008 <http://www.teenreads.com/reviews/9780316013680.asp>.

SIDEWALK. Interview with Sherman Alexie. 1999. 27 Feb. 2008 <http://www.fallsapart.com/art-side.html>.

SIMMONS, RUSSELL. *Russell Simmons Presents Def Poetry: Seasons 1–5.* Dir. Stan Lathan. Perf. Mos Def, Russell Simmons. HBO Home Video, 2002–2007.

SLAM. Dir. Marc Levin. Perf. Saul Williams, Sonja Sohn. Trimark Pictures Offline Entertainment Group, 1998.

SLAM NATION: THE SPORT OF SPOKEN WORD (1998). Dir. Paul Devlin. Perf. Mychele Dee, Jessica Care Moore. New Video Group-DVD, 2005.

SMITH, MARC KELLY, WITH JOE KRAYNAK. *The Complete Idiot's Guide to Slam Poetry.* New York: Alpha -Penguin, 2004.

SPENCER, RUSS. "What It Means to Be Sherman Alexie." *Book Magazine* (July/August 2000). 19 July 2005 <http://www.bookmagazine.com/archive/issue11/alexie.shtml>.

STRICKLAND, RENNARD. "Coyote Goes Hollywood." *Native Peoples Magazine* 13 Jan. 1997. 16 Sept. 2007 <http://www.nativepeoples.com/article/articles/174/1/COYOTE-GOES-HOLLYWOOD>.

SUSAG, DOROTHEA M. *Roots and Branches: A Resource of Native American Literature—Themes, Lessons, and Bibliographies.* Urbana, IL: National Council of Teachers of English, 1998.

THIEL, DIANE. "A Conversation with Sherman Alexie." *Crossroads, The Poetry Society of America Journal* (Spring 2004): 4–7. 17 Aug. 2007 <http://www.poetrysociety.org/journal/articles/salexie.html>.

TORREZ, JULIETTE. "Juliette Torrez Goes Long Distance with Sherman Alexie." (*Sic*) *Vice & Verse* 31 Aug. 1999. Sept. 2005 <http://poetry.about.com/library/weekly/aa083199.htm?once=true&terms =alexia>.

UMPHREY, CHRISTA. Editor's Introduction. *Montana Writing Project Journal.* 1.4 (2007): 3. <http://www.cas.umt.edu/english/mwp/documents/journal_july_07.pdf>.

VERNA, PAUL. "Don Speaks about Plans for Walden and the Thoreau Institute." *Billboard* New York, 1997. 14 July 2005.

VIDAL, GORE. *Screening History.* Cambridge: Harvard U P, 1992.

VIZENOR, GERALD, ED. *Narrative Chance: Postmodern Discourse on Native American Indian Literatures.* Norman: U of Oklahoma P, 1993.

WALSH, MIA. "A Taste of Life on the Rez." Rev. of *The Absolutely True Diary of a Part-Time Indian,* by Sherman Alexie. *The Yakima Herald Republic* 23 Oct. 2007. 1 Feb. 2008 <http://www.yakima-herald.com/page/dis/299808924551587>.

WALSH, S. KIRK. "Time-Traveling Lessons for a Teenager on the Verge." *The New York Times* 25 April 2007. 1 Feb. 2008 <http://www.nytimes.com/2007/04/25/books/25wals.html?ex=1335153600&en=602734897653ab25&ei=5124&partner=permalink&exprod=permalink>.

WEAVER, JACE. *That the People Might Live: Native American Literatures and Native American Community*. New York: Oxford U P, 1997.

WEISS, JEN, AND SCOTT HERNDON. *Brave New Voices: The YOUTH SPEAKS Guide to Teaching Spoken Word Poetry*. Portsmouth, NH: Heinemann, 2001.

WEST, DENNIS, AND JOAN WEST. "Sending Cinematic Smoke Signals: An Interview with Sherman Alexie." *Cineaste* 23.4 (1998): 28–32. 28 Jan. 2008 <http://www.lib.berkeley.edu/MRC/alexie.html>.

WIGET, ANDREW, ED. *Critical Essays on Native American Literature*. Boston: G. K. Hall, 1985.

———. *Dictionary of Native American Literature*. New York: Garland, 1994.

———. *Handbook of Native American Literature*. 1st ed. New York: Routledge, 1996.

———. *Native American Literature*. Boston: Twayne, 1985.

WILLIAMS, SARA T. "Alexie Tells Vivid Story Based on Own Ailment: '*Absolutely True Diary*' Is Author's First Fiction for Young Adults." *The Missoulian* 16 Sept. 2007: E2, E11.

WILTON, CAREN. "Native Son: The Sadness and Wit of Sherman Alexie." *The New Zealand Listener* 8–14 July 2006 [204.3452]. 20 Jan. 2008 <http://www.listener.co.nz/issue/3452/artsbooks/6485/native_son.html>.

WITALEC, JANET, JEFFREY CHAPMAN, AND CHRISTOPHER GIROUX, EDS. *Native North American Literature: Biographical and Critical Information on Native Writers and Orators from the United States and Canada from Historical Times to the Present*. New York: Gale Research, 1994.

WYRICK, KATHERINE H. "Common Cultures: Sherman Alexie Explores the Sacred and the Profane." Interview. *BookPage*. 2003. 13 Aug. 2006 <http://www.bookpage.com/0306bp/sherman_alexie.html>.

ZINN, HOWARD. *A People's History of the United States: 1492–Present*. New York: Perennial, 2003.

Authors

Heather E. Bruce is professor of English education at the University of Montana–Missoula and director of the Montana Writing Project. She previously taught English language arts for thirteen years in public schools at both the secondary and elementary levels. She is involved with pedagogical and curricular work that aims to address issues of access, relevance, and diversity for students living in poverty and with implementing Montana's legislative man- date: Indian Education for All. Her book *Literacies, Lies and Silences: Girls Writing Lives in the Classroom* (2003), an ethnographic analysis of women's studies student writers at Aspen Grove High School, examines the ways in which adolescents compose lives in the writing classroom. Other work has appeared in the NCTE volumes *Practice in Context* (2002) and *A Curriculum of Peace* (2004). Her articles have appeared in *English Journal, JAC,* and the *Quarterly Journal of the National Writing Project.* She is at work on *As If Our Lives Depended on Rhetoric: Social Justice Pedagogy in the Post-Civil Rights Era.*

Anna E. Baldwin teaches English at Arlee High School on the Flathead Indian Reservation in western Montana and also taught at Two Eagle River School, the tribal alternative school on the same reservation. She is a recipient of the Montana Office of Public Instruction's Ready-to-Go grants to develop teaching materials for Native American literature. She has presented teaching ideas for Native literature and other topics at numerous state and national conferences, and her articles and poems have appeared in the *English Journal* as well as the *Montana English Journal*.

Christabel Umphrey taught high school English, drama, and creative writing on the Flathead Indian Reservation in Ronan, Montana, for seven years. During this time, her classroom was a demonstration site, and she was a mentor teacher with the Montana Heritage Project, a statewide community-centered education program. She resigned in 2005 to complete her master's degree in English education and her library media endorsement while also teaching composition in the digital writing classroom at the University of Montana. She continues to live and work from her hometown on the reservation and is currently technology liaison for the Montana Writing Project, editor of the *Journal of the Montana Writing Project*, and editor of the *Montana English Journal*, the publication of the Montana Association of Teachers of English Language Arts (MATELA).